What people are saying about ...

Songs in the Key of Solomon

"These devotions won't put you to sleep. They may motivate you to do a few 'other things,' but sleep won't be one of them."

Gary and Karolyn Chapman, Gary is
the author of *The Five Love Languages*
and *The Five Languages of Apology*

"*Songs in the Key of Solomon* is not your typical couples' devotional. This book has a lighthearted approach to intimacy with a weighty perspective on its importance. Thanks, John and Anita, for your fresh approach to making life together better!"

Scott and Christine Dente, singers/
songwriters and recording artists

"What an innovative concept! John and Anita tap into the motivation of each gender by mixing a little 'spiritual business with a whole lot of pleasure!' We are body, soul, and spirit—most devotionals forget the hands-on home-work (pun totally intended) that mixes the joy of God's Word into our intimate married lives. This is sure to make couples look forward to devotions—and the moments of fun that will definitely follow."

Pam and Bill Farrel, best-selling authors
of *Men Are Like Waffles, Women Are Like Spaghetti* and *Red Hot Monogamy*

duets

duets

Still in the Word
. . . Still in the Mood

John & Anita Renfroe

David C Cook

transforming lives together

DUETS
Published by David C. Cook
4050 Lee Vance View
Colorado Springs, CO 80918 U.S.A.

David C. Cook Distribution Canada
55 Woodslee Avenue, Paris, Ontario, Canada N3L 3E5

David C. Cook U.K., Kingsway Communications
Eastbourne, East Sussex BN23 6NT, England

David C. Cook and the graphic circle C logo
are registered trademarks of Cook Communications Ministries.

Unless otherwise noted, all Scripture quotations are taken from *THE MESSAGE*.
Copyright © by Eugene H. Peterson 1993, 1994, 1995, 1996, 2000, 2001, 2002.
Used by permission of NavPress Publishing Group. Scripture quotations marked AB are
taken from *The Amplified Bible*. Copyright © 1954, 1958, 1962, 1964, 1965, 1987
by The Lockman Foundation. Used by permission; NIV are taken from the *Holy Bible,
New International Version®. NIV®*. Copyright © 1973, 1978, 1984 by International
Bible Society. Used by permission of Zondervan. All rights reserved; NASB are taken
from the *New American Standard Bible*, © Copyright 1960, 1995 by The Lockman
Foundation. Used by permission; NCV are taken from the New Century Version®.
Copyright © 1987, 1988, 1991 by Word Publishing, a division of Thomas Nelson,
Inc. Used by permission. All rights reserved; and NLT are taken from the New Living
Translation of the Holy Bible. New Living Translation copyright © 1996, 2004 by
Tyndale Charitable Trust. Used by permission of Tyndale House Publishers.

LCCN 2009937468
Hardcover ISBN 978-1-4347-6543-7
International Trade Paperback Edition ISBN 978-1-4347-0059-9
eISBN 978-1-4347-0081-0

The Team: Don Pape, Susan Tjaden, Sarah Schultz, Jack Campbell, and Susan Vannaman
Cover Design: Amy Kiechlin
Cover Photo: Sandy Ujfalusy, Strong Tower Photography

Printed in Canada
First Edition 2010

1 2 3 4 5 6 7 8 9 10

101509

For Seattle
who has provided us
with fresh perspective on legacy

Contents

overture

I f you are a normal couple (okay, stop for a moment— look at each other and laugh) … *ahem … perhaps we should start over.*

If you are a married couple, you have on occasion pondered whether or not you are doing this whole "married" thing right. You may sometimes think, *I bet we are the only couple who* _____ (fill in the blank with the behavior, situation, or problem du jour). Tucked inside that wondering is the seed of judgment that your marriage may be seriously lacking in the way that you and your spouse do life together. You look at other couples and think, *No one else seems to be struggling quite the way we are.*

And you feel isolated.

You feel *less than*.

You feel like you just can't get it right.

It's not particularly that you feel things are irreparable, or even broken for that matter. It's more like that gnawing feeling that you're not turning out to be the relational whiz you imagined yourself to be when you said, "I do."

Welcome to the club.

It's tough to keep the music playing in our marriage with all the other sounds vying for our attention and drowning out the rhythms that first drew us together. And it may have been so long since we heard the faint strains of love that they're a misty memory or sometimes difficult to remember at all. If you're newly married, the music may seem like it's not quite coming together as smoothly as you had envisioned, or if you're a little further along in your marital journey, you may have quit listening to the music altogether.

Which may lead you to wonder how this devotional book is going to help you, especially if you have already tried to find something that works for both of you. That was always the case with us. We wanted to find something that would speak to us at a heart level, would engage us together to talk about our lives, and would help us think about our lives in light of the Bible. We had never found a devotional that discussed the specifics of couples in the

Bible, and we thought maybe it was time to look at how they handled their marital business. Did the Bible just include the highlights that we're supposed to live up to? How did these couples fare? Face it, don't you wish there were TV shows like *The Bachelor: Jacob Finds a Wife* or *The Real Housewives of Canaan*?

There's a whole list of human beings in the Bible who struggled with the state of matrimony and a list of their less-than-stellar moments. It's kinda interesting that a book that begins with a man and a woman naked and unashamed in paradise unreels a series of couples with issues that (surprisingly!) feel pretty current and familiar. We are ever so grateful that the writers of Scripture did not spare us the difficult moments in these couples' lives throughout history. Their stories are told in all their glaring humanity. And by this we know that we are not alone.

We hope the format of the devotionals will be a sort of springboard for discussions that will encourage you and challenge you and bring real change (for the better!) to your marriage. We have chosen a biblical snapshot of each couple (for some, several snapshots) to give you a window into their marriage. Then we serve up a little commentary on how we view the situation. This in itself may cause some rousing discussion and debate, which we welcome! (Feel free to disagree with us! It's a free country!) We then categorize this snapshot as a "high note" or "low note" (that is, an example of a good relationship/interaction/situation or a not-so-good one) and share points for consideration in your own marriage. Finally, we give you "your duet" section, which includes an assignment (don't worry, they're mostly fun) or an opportunity to pray together about the subject matter at hand. Guys, don't worry: There are no relationship quizzes or questionnaires.

Of course, the criteria back in Bible times for strong, lasting, and great marriages were culturally quite different than they are for our generation. We are conditioned to believe that *great love stories equal lots of romance*. There's some of that included, but there were many arranged marriages and lots of multiple-wives situations in the Bible. For this devotional, though, we are mostly dealing with the scenario we are most familiar with—one man, one woman, long term. For many of these couples we see only a snapshot, one or two windows into their entire story. Sometimes we don't even know the wife's name (in those cases we generically call her Mrs. Whatever-the-Husband's-Name-Is). We really don't get to see much of the success or failure on either side of the slice of their lives revealed in Scripture. In fact, sometimes our only telling clue of their relationship is that they had children and died! (Talk about reducing it to "just the facts, ma'am"!) But the Bible does give us some pieces of their stories, and we can look for the parallels in our marriages today.

These stories, these couples, these *duets* sing their songs uniquely. Not perfectly—but that is how we know that we will not escape missteps, either. Many of these duets serve as cautionary tales. As British author Catherine Aird said, "If you can't be a good example, you'll just have to serve as a horrible warning." And there are plenty of those in Scripture. But a few couples and stories stand out as duets that brought moments of purity and clarity and harmony. Let those couples encourage you to know that such moments may resound in your marriage, and that may be your lasting legacy.

So how *do* we cut through the clutter of our everyday lives and hone in on the song that our souls were meant to sing together? How do we find our harmony, our unique duet? Perhaps a look at these couples and scenes from their lives can fine-tune our hearts.

one

Made for Each Other

Adam and Eve
(part one)

listen

GOD said, "It's not good for the Man to be alone;
I'll make him a helper, a companion." So GOD formed
from the dirt of the ground all the animals of the field
and all the birds of the air. He brought them to the
Man to see what he would name them. Whatever the
Man called each living creature, that was its name.
The Man named the cattle, named the birds of the air,

named the wild animals; but he didn't find a suitable companion.

GOD put the Man into a deep sleep. As he slept he removed one of his ribs and replaced it with flesh. GOD then used the rib that he had taken from the Man to make Woman and presented her to the Man. (Gen. 2:18–22)

our part

This is a great moment in marital history. Actually, the first one ever! And it was done with perfection, in perfection, by perfection. Take note. It was beautiful. And as we know, it was oh so fleeting. But for a while it was amazing—a taste of what it was supposed to be.

God gave Adam a job. There were a million species, and they all needed names. He had a lot to do, so things were good on the career front. Apparently busyness was not the same as fulfillment and satisfaction—even in a perfect job situation—because Adam was lonely despite being really busy.

It is interesting to note that God gave partners to all

the animals but waited for Adam to acknowledge his desire for a mate before He fashioned one for him. So God not only said that it was not good for man to dwell in isolation (How will he ever find matching socks? Who will let him know when to trim his nose hair?), but He also came up with a beautiful solution. God created Eve for Adam. She was not one of a million, she was couture—handmade, custom designed, and presented to him.

We all need someone to share with—our lives, our work, our thoughts and feelings, our destiny. This was a couple destined to make history. All of it.

high note or low note?

It was a stellar moment in the establishment of marriage. Unfortunately it was literally *all* downhill from there. Seems that one week in paradise is about all anyone can take. This was the only point in the history of all humanity that we could rate this marriage a perfect 10.

your part

We usually have to feel our loneliness deeply before we come to the conclusion that we are willing to do the work it takes to be in a marriage relationship for life. Explain to your partner the loneliness you experienced before they entered your life. Or perhaps share a moment when you were apart and something happened that you knew would be impossible to describe and your only wish was for them to be standing there witnessing it with you.

your duet

Make plans to view the sunset together tomorrow (or maybe tonight). Imagine how difficult it would be to capture the beauty of a sunset if you tried to explain it to each other in words. Some things just have to be shared and experienced.

two

Go Along, Get Along, Get It Wrong

Adam and Eve
(part two)

listen

GOD commanded the Man, "You can eat from any tree in the garden, except from the Tree-of-Knowledge-of-Good-and-Evil. Don't eat from it. The moment you eat from that tree, you're dead."

The serpent was clever, more clever than any wild animal GOD had made. He spoke to the Woman: "Do I understand that God told you not to eat from any tree in the garden?"

The Woman said to the serpent, "Not at all. We can eat from the trees in the garden. It's only about the tree in the middle of the garden that God said, 'Don't eat from it; don't even touch it or you'll die.'"

The serpent told the Woman, "You won't die. God knows that the moment you eat from that tree, you'll see what's really going on. You'll be just like God, knowing everything, ranging all the way from good to evil."

When the Woman saw that the tree looked like good eating and realized what she would get out of it—she'd know everything!—she took and ate the fruit and then gave some to her husband, and he ate. (Gen. 2:16–17, 3:1–6)

our part

There is much debate (by people smarter than we are) over who was with whom, and who knew what when, in the don't-touch-the-fruit story—but, regardless, the outcome is the same. The woman went along with the snake, and the man went along with the woman. Plainly, there was much going along.

You know the phrase "go along to get along," right? It means to make compromises for the sake of ease, to shut your mouth and just do whatever is necessary to avoid an argument. You weigh the amount of time it would take to discuss (heatedly, most likely) the issue at stake. Then you factor in how much time and energy you have on hand to devote to said "conversational-growth opportunity" and the inevitable cooling-off period—not to mention the likelihood of "no sugar tonight in your coffee" (obscure The Guess Who reference). Ultimately you come up with the notion that *it just might not be worth arguing.*

But there are times when the "go along to get along" approach is just plain wrong. Sometimes we need to strive with each other over matters. We need to create an environment where lively, heated discussion over *matters that matter* is not only okay, but is also viewed as healthy—necessary, even—to protect each other and our marriage from devastating decisions. This type of environment safeguards our marriage, especially when one of us feels strongly about the morality of an issue.

high note or low note?

Low. Avoiding confrontation is not always the most peaceable option.

your part

Calmly discuss how you each approach the decision about whether to confront the other or to not rock the boat. Why do you feel that certain topics are difficult to discuss with your beloved? Have there been situations where it would have been *more loving* to confront than to just go along?

your duet

Take a piece of paper and write each other a permission slip to "rock the boat" in a situation where your spouse might otherwise be afraid to do so. Tuck the slip away someplace safe (maybe the back of your wallet?) and don't be afraid to use it—for *good*.

three

Leaving, Cleaving, and Stuck on You

Adam and Eve
(part three)

listen

The Man said, "Finally! Bone of my bone, flesh of my flesh! Name her Woman for she was made from Man." Therefore a man leaves his father and mother and embraces his wife. They become one flesh. (Gen. 2:23–24)

our part

How great is it that Adam began his declaration with "Finally!"? Isn't that the way it feels when you have spent far too much time looking for someone to spend your life with and then *BAM!* there they are? You do remember when all you wanted to do was begin your life with this person, wake up next to this person, and share every thought and feeling with this person, right? Can you tap into your memory banks and recall that feeling? That is the ball of emotions behind Adam's declaration of "Finally!" Settled, done, finito, over. This is it. She is it. Game over.

Except for one thing.... Adam also has to come up with a name for her kind of species. The list is pretty short as there is only one name for the species (*man*). So he just tags on a prefix and she becomes *woman*. (It doesn't say that Eve discussed it, but we're pretty sure she might have had an opinion if she were not still under the effects of divine anesthesia.)

The verses following that event inform us that Adam and Eve established the important principles of leaving their families (interesting, given that there were no families to leave, as of yet). But if you really look at the root causes

of a lot of marital difficulty, it will often come in one of
these three areas they identified:

1. Leaving: One of the partners cannot separate fully
   from their family of origin.

2. Cleaving: Just as "aloha" can mean both hello *and*
   good-bye, "cleave" can mean both to separate *and*
   to attach (say good-bye to the old, hello to the
   new). It is somewhat like a trapeze artist who must
   fully let go of one bar in order to grab and hold
   the other. If you try to hold on to one bar while
   trying to grasp the next, you will be torn in two
   directions and painfully stuck in midair.

3. Becoming one flesh: This means being intimate.
   Knowing each other in ways that are deeply
   personal and sexual, as no one else can know you,
   and determining to be that way always.

high note or low note?

This is taking place before the fall, so all the notes were
pretty high. They show us what it's like to be intimate and
exclusive. And appreciative.

your part

Okay. Gut-level-honesty time. Give your partner permission to speak freely about how they feel your marriage is measuring up in these three test areas: leaving, cleaving, one flesh-ing. Listen with your heart, and speak the truth in love. Together decide on some new ways to step up your game in any areas that need shoring up.

your duet

Pray for your partner and your marriage, that you can see the places where there may be a foundational crack in the leave/cleave/unity trifecta. The ability to see it and work together on it is critical to the health and longevity of your union.

Exposed

Adam and Eve
(part four)

listen

When the Woman saw that the tree looked like good eating and realized what she would get out of it—she'd know everything!—she took and ate the fruit and then gave some to her husband, and he ate.

Immediately the two of them did "see what's really going on"—saw themselves naked! They sewed fig

leaves together as makeshift clothes for themselves.
(Gen. 3:6–7)

our part

Eve knew a good thing when she saw it. Well, a good-looking thing at least. She also realized the upside to knowledge: She would be *more knowledgeable*. What possible harm could that do? Isn't knowledge power? And who wouldn't want to be more powerful? Perhaps God may have overstated the consequences. He's loving toward His creation, right? And Adam will want to share this experience, right? But all her reasoning and persuading led them to a place they never desired to be: exposed.

One thing's for sure: Marriage will expose you. Living with someone 24–7 will bring out the good, the bad, and the ugly. We all attempt that "best foot forward" approach when dating, but life together will lay it all bare. The decisions you make as a couple will always lead you either closer to God or farther away. It seems there should be some sort of middle ground where there is "marital stasis," but there isn't. Adam and Eve started out in the garden of Eden naked and unashamed (true intimacy) and ended up naked and aware (knowledgeable and miserable). Some things you would rather not share, and in those moments you feel exposed.

It seems that they were also engaged in something that we will witness in other marriages in the Bible: the attempted cover-up. Nothing expresses our human reaction to exposure like our instinct to hide. We try to hide from God. We try to hide from each other emotionally and keep our failures tightly under wraps, all the while suffocating the life out of our relationship, killing true intimacy. While we are sewing fig leaves of fear, God offers us a true covering of forgiveness (Gen. 3:21). Isn't it time that we come clean with each other … and with God?

high note or low note?

You can see how this would be a very, very low note. And the beginning of all marital low notes to come. Forever.

your part

Talk about a time in your childhood when you thought you had pulled a fast one on your parents but you got busted. Did you hide from your parents? What were you trying to hide?

It's difficult to come out of our hiding places. We are comfortable there, yet, on many levels, miserable with our pathetic "fig leaves" (busyness, workaholism, perfectionism, deception, addictions, noncommunication). It takes a good bit of coaxing from God to realize what exactly we are hiding and who we think we are hiding it from. God knows who you are and where you are and what you are hiding. Your fig leaves are about as effective as wearing a cotton T-shirt in an X-ray machine. It may make you feel covered up, but it's hiding nothing.

Do you desire to be truly intimate with God and with your spouse? It takes courage and risk. You may not be able to discuss this right away, but make a commitment to consider at least one fig leaf you are ready to exchange for forgiveness in your life.

your duet

Ask God to help you, as a couple, to make decisions that lead you in a God-ward direction together, and for the wisdom to see the fig leaves you hide behind regularly.

When the Honeymoon Is Definitely Over

Adam and Eve
(part five)

listen

Then the man—Adam—named his wife Eve,
because she would be the mother of all who live. And
the LORD God made clothing from animal skins for
Adam and his wife.

Then the LORD God said, "Look, the human beings
have become like us, knowing both good and evil.
What if they reach out, take fruit from the tree of life,
and eat it? Then they will live forever!" So the LORD
God banished them from the Garden of Eden, and
he sent Adam out to cultivate the ground from which
he had been made. After sending them out, the LORD
God stationed mighty cherubim to the east of the
Garden of Eden. And he placed a flaming sword that
flashed back and forth to guard the way to the tree of
life. (Gen. 3:20–24 NLT)

our part

In the space-travel spoof *Galaxy Quest,* there is an
intergalactic struggle for possession of a device that
reorganizes molecules so that you can go back in time
thirteen seconds and undo any ill-informed, stupid, or
catastrophic thing that had happened. That would come
in handy, wouldn't it? If only to change some lame thing
you said, or to stop yourself before you ate the whole tray
of nachos, or to give yourself another chance to turn a
little wider at the bank drive-through to avoid scraping

your paint job. Think about it: Thirteen seconds ago you weren't such an idiot. Don't you know Adam and Eve would have loved to have gotten their hands on that device? But perfection doesn't last. Period. No one may have experienced this more graphically than the only (temporarily) perfect couple. After they were sent packing from their perfect paradise, God placed a strong visual reminder that they could never go back and undo their life-altering decision. There was no return to their former perfect life.

Time runs in only one direction and, no matter how much we wish we could return to the point of decision or action, it is as if cherubim are placed at the entry to What Was, leaving only one direction to move: forward, together. Without the unfailing mercies of the Lord in our lives, we are stuck staring at the cherubim and the flaming sword, wondering how we messed up so royally. But because of the unfailing mercies of the Lord, we look out at the land that lies a little outside the bounds of perfection and know that we can make it. Together.

high note or low note?

Somewhere in the middle. Perfection was lost. Togetherness in spite of imperfection was achieved, though.

your part

If you could get your hands on that device from *Galaxy Quest,* what thirteen-second molecular rearrangement would you like to have revisited? What life lessons and deep bonds of trust would you lose or gain if you could have changed things?

your duet

Ask God to help you see the cherubim and flaming swords marking your life and to help you look forward rather than backward.

six

The Apple Doesn't Fall

Adam and Eve
(part six)

listen

Adam slept with his wife again. She had a son whom she named Seth. She said, "God has given me another child in place of Abel whom Cain killed." And then Seth had a son whom he named Enosh.

That's when men and women began praying and worshiping in the name of GOD. (Gen. 4:25–26)

our part

You know the phrase "the apple doesn't fall far from the tree"? In the case of Adam and Eve, their family had a rough start. There was the Original Sin, with the resulting curse of frustrating work and pain in childbirth. There was the first-ever homicide/fratricide (and you couldn't even blame it on bad peer groups, negative cultural influences, or violent video games) along with the residual memories of how they had it all and lost it. If Adam and Eve harbored a great deal of blame between themselves for what had happened and had difficulty believing that they had once walked and talked with God in the garden and now could not, who could really blame them?

Perhaps their children? Wouldn't the kids just be mimicking the stories they heard their parents recite about blaming each other for the fruit? So here we have the first "apple doesn't fall" cautionary tale. Seems that neither Adam nor Eve nor their children could find a way to interact with God. They had to wait until the next generation came along before man would start seeking God. It wasn't until the time of Enosh that we hear the description that people "began praying and worshiping."

It is sobering to see that the decisions we make as a couple will certainly imprint (positively or negatively) our family's ability and desire to seek God.

high note or low note?

It seemed that Adam and Eve couldn't get any lower, but obviously they did since they took the kids down with them.

your part

Take a few moments to talk about your family of origin and how their influence has either made it more difficult to grow in your spiritual life *or* created a desire to know and follow God. That doesn't necessarily mean that you have to follow in their footsteps, but you can't deny that there is much power in the foundational imprints of our lives. If you are parents, talk about how you believe you are imprinting your children.

your duet

How much do you know about your family tree? This might be a good time to investigate your spiritual heritage.

Sit down together and create one on a sheet of paper. It doesn't have to be beautiful or elaborate, but fill in as many blanks as you can. Then ask your relatives what kind of spiritual life your ancestors may have had.

seven

Disemb-ark-ing

Noah and Mrs. Noah
(part one)

listen

> *But I will confirm my covenant with you. So enter the boat—you and your wife and your sons and their wives. Bring a pair of every kind of animal—a male and a female—into the boat with you to keep them alive during the flood. (Gen. 6:18–19 NLT)*

"Leave the boat, all of you—you and your wife, and your sons and their wives. Release all the animals—the birds, the livestock, and the small animals that scurry along the ground—so they can be fruitful and multiply throughout the earth."

So Noah, his wife, and his sons and their wives left the boat. (Gen. 8:16–18 NLT)

our part

Reading the two passages above, which do you think took more faith: believing that God was going to do something catastrophic that required the building of an ark *or* getting off the boat and trusting that God wasn't going to do it again?

The images of that kind of large-scale devastation would be hard to shake. Big changes in our lives can knock us off our centers and leave us reeling and unable to find a solid place to land. The torrential rains that covered the earth lasted forty days, but Noah and his family stayed adrift on the boat for seven months, and they couldn't even see the tops of the mountains for *another* three months. They were on the floating zoo barge for an entire year. And then came the day when they had to trust enough to step off the boat. They were not *hypothetically* the only family left on earth; they were *literally* so. Would they be lonely? Would the earth be the same one they had known before? How would their lives be fundamentally changed?

If you, as a couple, have been through a life-altering event together, you can attest to the levels of trepidation you experience when you are preparing to reenter the realm of the everyday. You know that life will never be as it was before, but you also know that you cannot remain on the "ark" forever. It was never meant to be a permanent place to live.

high note or low note?

Noah and the missus show us that they could stay loose and obedient in the face of changing life circumstances. When all they had ever known was gone forever, they still were a family.

your part

Have you been at this point as a couple? Where you had to trust that—despite the life-altering circumstance (job loss, illness, infertility, death in the family, or whatever else)—God was still there, asking you to step away from the safety of your temporary shelter to return to a world where very little looked recognizable? If so, did you feel that this situation brought you closer together or spread you farther apart? What sorts of things can you build into your marriage *now* that will benefit you when these things happen the next time? (And they invariably will.)

your duet

Thank God for the fact that you are together, despite the things you have been through that could have torn you apart. Ask God to help you strengthen your marriage now for whatever roads you will walk together in the future.

eight

So I Have This Idea ...

Noah and Mrs. Noah
(part two)

listen

*Noah was 600 years old when the flood covered
the earth. He went on board the boat to escape the
flood—he and his wife and his sons and their wives.
With them were all the various kinds of animals—
those approved for eating and for sacrifice and those
that were not—along with all the birds and the small
animals that scurry along the ground. They entered*

> *the boat in pairs, male and female, just as God had*
> *commanded Noah. After seven days, the waters of the*
> *flood came and covered the earth. (Gen. 7:6–10 NLT)*

our part

Sometimes it's hard for your spouse to sell you on their dream. Sure you love them. Sure you believe in them. Sure you are devoted to their happiness. But to be a receptive listener to your mate's kinda far-out ideas takes a bundle of skills. It requires a certain suspension of all you know about them, a commitment to not laugh out loud when they mention some harebrained idea that can only be explained as something they "really need to do." Such was the case with Mrs. Noah. If you read Genesis 5, you see that Mr. Noah was about five hundred years old when he became a father for the first time (insert your own punch line here) and received word that this crazy boat-building project was something that the Lord wanted him to do. Exactly how does one pitch such an idea to his significant other? "Honey, God told me to build something no one has ever built before to float on something no one has ever witnessed before. And I really need your support, okay?"

Then he worked on this in his backyard for *one hundred years!* Now we realize that either people lived a lot longer back then, or they counted years differently than we do now, but no matter. The point is he was working on this for a significant chunk of time.

Consider how long it seems when you are working on vacation plans; now add to that the amount of time it would take you to build the ship you had to use to cruise there. This is a level of spousal support that is truly heroic. The fact that Mrs. Noah did not leave him high and dry (pun torture) is a testament to the strength of her love and commitment. And—eventually—it paid off, as she got to survive and help start the whole world over.

high note or low note?

Definitely high. Legendary patience with a spouse's midlife career change or passionate hobby may need to be more associated with Mrs. Noah than Mr. Job.

your part

Talk about different pursuits that may have put you in the "Mrs. Noah" spot a time or two. There are times in every marriage when you have to cash in a few of the "trust chips" you have accrued in order to buy a little belief in the project/calling/mission du jour. How can we make sure we are showing faith in each other in ways that matter to the other person?

your duet

Okay, so we don't know if Mrs. Noah was out there with a hammer and nails on the gopher wood, but we do know that couples who work on projects together learn a lot about each other. It also allows for times to learn how to appreciate the talents and work styles of your partner. There is a sense of mutual accomplishment and a sense that you could do just about anything if you put your collective minds to it. Or, it will be a total wreck and you will have something to laugh about together. Either way, pick something you think you might like to work on together and put it on the calendar. And just hope that it won't take a hundred years.

nine

Moving Day

Abram and Sarai
(part one)

listen

The LORD had said to Abram, "Leave your country,
your people and your father's household and go to the
land I will show you.

"I will make you into a great nation
*   and I will bless you;*

> *I will make your name great,*
> *and you will be a blessing.*
> *I will bless those who bless you,*
> *and whoever curses you I will curse;*
> *and all peoples on earth*
> *will be blessed through you."*

> *So Abram left, as the LORD had told him; and Lot*
> *went with him. Abram was seventy-five years old when*
> *he set out from Haran. He took his wife Sarai, his*
> *nephew Lot, all the possessions they had accumulated*
> *and the people they had acquired in Haran, and they*
> *set out for the land of Canaan, and they arrived there.*
> *(Gen. 12:1–5 NIV)*

our part

Here we have our first real example of the "leave and cleave" principle: "[Abram] took his wife Sarai … and they set out."

There is always a lot of angst that comes with a move. Usually one person in the marriage is a little more excited than the other. It's hard enough to move when you're young and energetic and don't have a lot of stuff. It's much more complicated when you have deep roots in a community and your attic is full of years of memories and stuff you just can't bring yourself to throw away.

But Abram had a promise. He did not have an heir or an address yet, but he and God had a real relationship that included Abram listening while God talked, and then God listening while Abram talked. Neither of them thought this was strange. And one day God told Abram that he would have to trust Him. He would have to pick up the Mayflower moving truck but leave the drop-off address blank. And he would have to convince the family that this was a good thing. It is not recorded in Scripture just how Sarai took it. We wonder if she protested and wailed and went anyway, or if she silently suffered as she packed, or if perhaps she was a willing relocator. Regardless, she is listed in the Hebrews passage (alongside her husband) with all the people who exhibited extraordinary faith. They were a unit, and Sarai took Abram's hand to walk into their destiny.

high note or low note?

We don't know Sarai's level of willingness, but she went. Let's all hope that when history is recorded, we will be judged on our actions and not all the discussion it took to get to there.

your part

How many times have you moved in your married life? Was there one that was particularly painful because you had to uproot where the roots were deep? Did your marriage flourish in the new place, or did you leave part of your heart behind? What have been the net gains for your marriage in your various moves?

your duet

Take out a map of your country or a map of the world (or click an app on your iPhone if you are just that cool), and show your spouse where you would want to live if you knew that there would be no negative financial impact on your family and you knew that your spouse would go with you. Explain why you selected this location.

ten

Well ... Not Exactly ...

Abram and Sarai
(part two)

listen

Now there was a famine in the land, and Abram went down to Egypt to live there for a while because the famine was severe. As he was about to enter Egypt, he said to his wife Sarai, "I know what a beautiful woman you are. When the Egyptians see you, they will say, 'This is his wife.' Then they will kill me but will let you live. Say you are my sister, so that I will be treated well for your sake and my life will be spared because of you."

When Abram came to Egypt, the Egyptians saw that she was a very beautiful woman. And when Pharaoh's officials saw her, they praised her to Pharaoh, and she was taken into his palace. He treated Abram well for her sake, and Abram acquired sheep and cattle, male and female donkeys, menservants and maidservants, and camels.

But the LORD inflicted serious diseases on Pharaoh and his household because of Abram's wife Sarai. So Pharaoh summoned Abram. "What have you done to me?" he said. "Why didn't you tell me she was your wife? Why did you say, 'She is my sister,' so that I took her to be my wife? Now then, here is your wife. Take her and go!" Then Pharaoh gave orders about Abram to his men, and they sent him on his way, with his wife and everything he had. (Gen. 12:10–20 NIV)

our part

It didn't take long in the development of civilization for the first case of situational ethics to affect a marriage. There are times when you are willing to make sacrifices to help the cause, but there are occasions when you are asked to go beyond what you know to be the truth. You can write this down: *It will not end well.*

Abram may have talked with God, but more than once in the Scriptures he blew it with the "you are too beautiful for my own good so lie a little won't you please" scenario. He didn't mind letting Sarai dwell in the palace of the pharaoh while he was off on his get-rich-quick scheme in Egypt, and it took the heathen ruler to point out the error of the patriarch's ways. Talk about a public humiliation! It's tough enough to be called out for lying, but to get kicked out of the country for being an accomplice must have shamed Sarai, too. They were lucky to be spared their lives. It would be great to say that they learned their lesson here, but later they tried to pull the same shenanigan again with the same results (Gen. 20).

Some situations require creative problem solving, but your life and marriage will always suffer when you jettison your morals for the convenience of the moment.

high note or low note?

Collusion for the purposes of deception is never a high-water mark in any marriage. (See also Isaac and Rebekah, and Ananias and Sapphira.)

your part

How are crises of morals and conscience dealt with in your marriage? Is there permission to dissent freely with issues? Is there a clear standard regarding honest/dishonest, moral/immoral, right/wrong that you both adhere to, or are there many gray areas that keep working their way up to the surface as situations force them? Has this cost you personally? Your marriage?

your duet

Consider this a moment to solidify your commitment, as a couple, to truth: with each other, with your family, in your financial dealings, and in your business decisions. Somehow we allow ourselves to believe that these things don't affect our marriage, but they always do.

eleven

The Waiting Is the Hardest Part

Abram and Sarai
(part three)

listen

Now Sarai, Abram's wife, had borne him no children. She had an Egyptian maid whose name was Hagar.

And Sarai said to Abram, See here, the Lord has restrained me from bearing [children]. I am asking

*you to have intercourse with my maid; it may be that I
can obtain children by her. And Abram listened to and
heeded what Sarai said.*

*So Sarai, Abram's wife, took Hagar her Egyptian
maid, after Abram had dwelt ten years in the land of
Canaan, and gave her to her husband Abram to be his
[secondary] wife.*

*And he had intercourse with Hagar, and she became
pregnant; and when she saw that she was with child,
she looked with contempt upon her mistress and
despised her.*

*Then Sarai said to Abram, May [the responsibility
for] my wrong and deprivation of rights be upon
you! I gave my maid into your bosom, and when
she saw that she was with child, I was contemptible
and despised in her eyes. May the Lord be the judge
between you and me.*

But Abram said to Sarai, See here, your maid is in your hands and power; do as you please with her. And when Sarai dealt severely with her, humbling and afflicting her, she [Hagar] fled from her. (Gen. 16:1–6 AB)

our part

As the old song says, "The waiting is the hardest part."

We are an impatient race, we humans. We get a vision for something that we know is God-given, but cannot seem to wait well enough to see it come to pass. We may feel as though we have fallen off God's radar or like He may have forgotten what He promised us. Or perhaps *(ding)* He may need a skosh of our assistance. Maybe we can help move this thing along. We have a "better plan," a "faster route," an "improved method."

Looking back at Sarai's debacle, it's easy to Monday-morning quarterback, but when we are in a situation that seems like it's not going anywhere, there is a distinct temptation to take matters into our own hands. We offer our best human rationale, our most logical deductions, and we come up with the perfect *un*solution: something that makes things infinitely and generationally worse than they would have been if we had merely waited. And when we finally do get what we thought we wanted, it is rife with resentment and hatred. Middle East–epic battles that go on for eons ensue. All this from our desire to "assist" God in His plan and His timing.

Although the song says that the waiting is the hardest part, it might just be that offering our own unsolution is harder after all.

high note or low note?
Low and long term. This situation was the genesis of a divide in politics and religion that persists in our world even today.

your part
As hard as it is to believe that something as benign as simple impatience might be the thing that sets a series of disastrous consequences in motion, it certainly can. What are you waiting for in your life? In your marriage? Are there things that you believe are a part of your future that aren't coming quite quickly enough and you are starting to

wonder if God's timing may be questionable? How can we shore up each other's patience quotient when it is wearing thin? How do we know the difference between waiting on God and refusing to take responsible action, when action is required of us? How do we know which is which?

your duet

Usually God puts a patient person together with an impatient one. It is maddening and balancing. Pray for each other with regard to your patience quotients. Acknowledge to God if this is an area you struggle with, and ask Him to help you learn to wait on Him (even when you feel that you have a way to shortcut His process).

Laughing Matters

Abram and Sarai
(part four)

listen

Overwhelmed, Abram fell flat on his face. Then
God said to him, "This is my covenant with you: You'll
be the father of many nations. Your name will no
longer be Abram, but Abraham, meaning that 'I'm
making you the father of many nations.' I'll make
you a father of fathers—I'll make nations from you,
kings will issue from you. I'm establishing my covenant

*between me and you, a covenant that includes your
descendants, a covenant that goes on and on and on,
a covenant that commits me to be your God and the
God of your descendants. And I'm giving you and your
descendants this land where you're now just camping,
this whole country of Canaan, to own forever. And I'll
be their God."*

*God continued speaking to Abraham, "And Sarai
your wife: Don't call her Sarai any longer; call her
Sarah. I'll bless her—yes! I'll give you a son by her! Oh,
how I'll bless her! Nations will come from her; kings of
nations will come from her."*

*Abraham fell flat on his face. And then he laughed,
thinking, "Can a hundred-year-old man father a son?
And can Sarah, at ninety years, have a baby?"*

*Abraham and Sarah were old by this time, very old.
Sarah was far past the age for having babies. Sarah
laughed within herself, "An old woman like me? Get
pregnant? With this old man of a husband?"*

GOD said to Abraham, "Why did Sarah laugh saying, 'Me? Have a baby? An old woman like me?' Is anything too hard for GOD? I'll be back about this time next year and Sarah will have a baby."

Sarah lied. She said, "I didn't laugh," because she was afraid.

But he said, "Yes you did; you laughed." (Gen. 17:5–6, 15–17; 18:11–15)

our part

If God was trying for some sort of witness protection program, changing a couple of vowels and consonants was not really that great of a plan. Yes, these were people who had not had the best streak of great decisions of late, but God is rich in mercy and continues to hold out the carrot of the future to a couple who seem to drift in and out of grasping the promises God had for them. The idea that this geriatric pair was going to produce viable offspring set them both into a fit of laughter, which shows that—regardless of their foibles—their sense of humor was still firmly intact. It's interesting that God only called Sarah up short for lying, not for laughing. When her son was born, she named him Isaac, which means "laughter" because she thought that all would laugh with her—like the whole world would appreciate the joke. There are many predictors of the longevity of a relationship, but one that is reported most frequently is an ability to laugh with each other. Really laugh. Loudly.

And often.

high note or low note?

God is still confident that He has chosen the right people for the job of fathering (and mothering) many nations—and the story ends with laughter. That's always a good thing.

your part

In our family we have people who are funny, people who think they're funny, people who know they aren't funny, and people who feel they alone adjudicate what is and isn't funny. But there is always lots of laughter in the house. On a scale of 0–10 (0 being no laughter, 10 being lots of daily laughter), how would you rate the laughter quotient in your house? Has it always been like this? Have there been circumstances that have impacted your laughter quotient rating recently?

your duet

Make a list of your Top Five Inside Jokes—you know, things that are funny between you and your spouse that absolutely no one else would understand or even think were the least bit funny.

Life in the Rearview Mirror

Lot and His Wife

listen

At dawn the next morning, the angels begged Lot to hurry. They said, "Go! Take your wife and your two daughters with you so you will not be destroyed when the city is punished."

But Lot delayed. So the two men took the hands of Lot, his wife, and his two daughters and led them safely out of the city. So the LORD was merciful to Lot and his family. After they brought them out of the city, one of the men said, "Run for your lives! Don't look back or stop anywhere in the valley. Run to the mountains, or you will be destroyed."

The sun had already come up when Lot entered Zoar. The LORD sent a rain of burning sulfur down from the sky on Sodom and Gomorrah and destroyed those cities. He also destroyed the whole Jordan Valley, everyone living in the cities, and even all the plants.

At that point Lot's wife looked back. When she did, she became a pillar of salt. (Gen. 19:15–17, 23–26 NCV)

our part

What is it about human nature that makes it so hard to let go of something? We have to be thrust from the womb to even begin our lives, and we tend to hang on to that which is familiar until we are practically pried from it for the rest of our days. Even when our comfort zone becomes decidedly *un*comfortable, it is still deemed preferable to the unknown zone. Lot and Mrs. Lot were assured of the certain destruction of their hometown by angelic beings, with the message coming straight from the God who was about to make it happen, and they were still reluctant to leave. They even had a warning about the temptation to stop for a moment of curiosity or regret. This is a situation where we see the distinct nature of marriage—each person is responsible for their own actions. Mrs. Lot became a salt lick, but Lot did not. We can't know what might have compelled her to turn around, but she was rescued from certain doom only to then choose it for herself.

high note or low note?

Left behind as a pile of NaCl? Regret is a luxury no marriage can afford.

your part

There's a difference between checking the rearview mirror for safety concerns and trying to drive your car forward while staring into the rearview mirror. How can we learn lessons from our past without camping out in the regret zone? Is one person in your marriage prone to get stuck there? Has this penchant for regret ever done anything positive for your marriage?

your duet

Ask God to help you both find constructive ways to view your past experiences without the lens of regret. He is willing to help us when we want to change the way we deal with the wrong choices of our past. You cannot build your future on a foundation of regret.

fourteen

Knock, Knock, Knockin' on Heaven's Door

Isaac and Rebekah
(part one)

listen

After the servant told Isaac the whole story of the trip, Isaac took Rebekah into the tent of his mother Sarah. He married Rebekah and she became his wife and he loved her. So Isaac found comfort after his mother's death.

*Isaac prayed hard to GOD for his wife because she
was barren. GOD answered his prayer and Rebekah
became pregnant. But the children tumbled and kicked
inside her so much that she said, "If this is the way it's
going to be, why go on living?" She went to GOD to
find out what was going on. GOD told her,*

> *Two nations are in your womb,
>   two peoples butting heads while still in your body.*
>
> *One people will overpower the other,
>   and the older will serve the younger.*

*When her time to give birth came, sure enough,
there were twins in her womb. The first came out
reddish, as if snugly wrapped in a hairy blanket; they
named him Esau (Hairy). His brother followed, his
fist clutched tight to Esau's heel; they named him Jacob
(Heel). Isaac was sixty years old when they were born.
(Gen. 24:66–67, 25:21–26)*

our part

Isaac loved his wife. His love was displayed by his persistent intercession for her. When Scripture tells us that Isaac prayed for her infertility and God answered his prayer, it *seems* like he prayed one day and she was pregnant the next. And that's unfortunate because it doesn't really show that things normally take much longer than a day to get resolved. In this case, though, it actually took twenty years. Twenty years of asking God for something. Wow.

We are so used to seeing television episodes and movies that wrap up everything in an hour or two, and we live in an era where quicker is always better and attention deficit disorders are more common than head colds. Twenty years of praying for one thing? That's persistence. That's love. When we pledge our love to our mate, we also promise that we will be the one who will champion their heart's desire and continue to pray for them no matter how long it takes to see an answer come to pass. And, just a side note: If you had twenty years to think about baby names, don't you think you would come up with something better than Hairy (Esau) and Heel (Jacob)?

high note or low note?

Persistent prayer for your spouse from a heart of love—the highest.

your part

The Bee Gees song asks, "How Deep Is Your Love?" and the answer just might lie in your willingness to go to God on your spouse's behalf and persist for them. For days, weeks, years. It's a different gesture of love than lavishing them with vacations and gifts and romantic dinners—but in the things that really matter in life, it's the only thing that counts forever. Are you ready to take on the long-term intercessor role for your beloved?

your duet

Share your deepest concerns/needs with each other. Pray for the ability to love your spouse in this most intimate way.

fifteen

Playing Favorites

Isaac and Rebekah
(part two)

listen

*When the boys grew up, Esau became a skilled
hunter. He loved to be out in the fields. But Jacob was
a quiet man and stayed among the tents. Isaac loved
Esau because he hunted the wild animals that Isaac
enjoyed eating. But Rebekah loved Jacob.*

[Isaac said to Esau,] "So take your bow and arrows and go hunting in the field for an animal for me to eat. When you prepare the tasty food that I love, bring it to me, and I will eat. Then I will bless you before I die." So Esau went out in the field to hunt.

Rebekah was listening as Isaac said this to his son Esau. She said to her son Jacob, "Listen, I heard your father saying to your brother Esau, 'Kill an animal and prepare some tasty food for me to eat. Then I will bless you in the presence of the LORD before I die.' So obey me, my son, and do what I tell you. Go out to our goats and bring me two of the best young ones. I will prepare them just the way your father likes them. Then you will take the food to your father, and he will bless you before he dies." (Gen. 25:27–28, 27:3–10 NCV)

our part

Nature abhors a vacuum. So do male drivers. If there's an inch between a bumper and a fender, they will fill it up. Relationships, also, abhor vacuums. If you leave a gap, something or someone will come and fill it up—and then our alliances shift and situations must be manipulated and ... oh what a tangled web we weave....

This is another variation on the "circle of trust" theme, but when we allow anyone to wedge between us (our friends, our career, our parents, even our children!), we end up in scenarios where we are playing each other for the upper hand. Yet there are no winners. Here are the offspring for which Isaac prayed twenty years, and they have now pitted their parents against each other for the coveted blessing (which seems trivial to us, but it was the position of leadership and financial benefit that would literally determine who was the familial head for the next generation—a lot was at stake!). Isaac and Rebekah had a massive failure to "cleave" once they started playing favorites with their kids. And a marriage that begins with a declaration of love and a commitment to prayer somehow can (with a failure to remember their primary relationship) still fumble on the one-yard line.

high note or low note?

A messy finish to a story that started so well.

your part

This passage reminds us of the continual vigilance we need in order to finish well. Relationships are never static—they are either moving toward more closeness and unity or away from it. Talk about the last two years of your marriage (if you've been married that long; if not, maybe just the last two months) and how you feel about this aspect: Is your circle of trust solid and strengthening, or are other issues creeping in and drawing you away from your primary commitment to each other?

your duet

Think of three couples who are much older than you (if you're in your nineties and reading this devotional, this may be difficult for you—then just think of peer couples who have been married a long time) and where they are in their journey. Do you feel that they are strong in their trust factors and on track to finish well?

sixteen

Déjà Vu All Over Again

Isaac and Rebekah
(part three)

listen

*And the men of the place asked him about his wife,
and he said, She is my sister; for he was afraid to say,
She is my wife—[thinking], Lest the men of the place
should kill me for Rebekah, because she is attractive
and is beautiful to look upon.*

When he had been there a long time, Abimelech
king of the Philistines looked out of a window and saw
Isaac caressing Rebekah his wife.

And Abimelech called Isaac and said, See here, she is
certainly your wife! How did you [dare] say to me, She
is my sister? And Isaac said to him, Because I thought,
Lest I die on account of her.

And Abimelech said, What is this you have done to us?
One of the men might easily have lain with your wife,
and you would have brought guilt and sin upon us.

Then Abimelech charged all his people, He who
touches this man or his wife shall surely be put to
death. (Gen. 26:7–11 AB)

our part

Sound familiar? Daddy Abraham drew up this little
scenario when he was in a tight spot in a foreign land—
with the same outcome. We may say that we abhor the
role models we grew up with, yet it is easy to fall into the

same default setting when we aren't intentional about our underlying motives or are faced with an intense situation.

That whole "sins of the fathers" phrase speaks to the generational weaknesses we both create and fall back on. Every choice we make as a couple is reinforced by the fact that it was thought up by one party and ratified by the other—in effect, doubling the strength of the decision. This is powerful when it is harnessed for the things in our lives that build our integrity and character, but it also magnifies the intensity of our wrong choices. We do not live in a vacuum, spiritually or generationally. Every decision we make needs to be run through the filter of "legacy" and not just based on the convenience of the moment. What's right will always be right. What's wrong will usually be repeated.

high note or low note?

Returning to family default position under pressure—easy and low.

your part

What have your parents given you as a family default position when you are under pressure? Discuss if you feel it is easy or difficult to overcome the negative ones ("I will never be like _____!") or if you find yourself returning to the behavior that you, in theory, disagree with.

your duet

Take a moment to imagine if your family had been included in Scripture. What would your family's legacy have been reduced to? What would be the standout moments? What "crash and burn" segments might have to be included? What would be the lessons for your children's children's children?

seventeen

Overtime

Jacob and Rachel
(part one)

listen

Then Laban said to Jacob, "You are my relative,
but it is not right for you to work for me without pay.
What would you like me to pay you?"

Jacob loved Rachel, so he said to Laban, "Let me
marry your younger daughter Rachel. If you will, I will
work seven years for you."

Laban said, "It would be better for her to marry
you than someone else, so stay here with me." So
Jacob worked for Laban seven years so he could marry
Rachel. But they seemed like just a few days to him
because he loved Rachel very much.

After seven years Jacob said to Laban, "Give me
Rachel so that I may marry her. The time I promised to
work for you is over."

So Laban gave a feast for all the people there.
That evening he brought his daughter Leah to Jacob,
and they had sexual relations. (Laban gave his slave
girl Zilpah to his daughter to be her servant.) In the
morning when Jacob saw that he had had sexual
relations with Leah, he said to Laban, "What have
you done to me? I worked hard for you so that I could
marry Rachel! Why did you trick me?"

Laban said, "In our country we do not allow the
younger daughter to marry before the older daughter.
But complete the full week of the marriage ceremony

with Leah, and I will give you Rachel to marry also.
But you must serve me another seven years."

So Jacob did this, and when he had completed the
week with Leah, Laban gave him his daughter Rachel
as a wife. (Gen. 29:15, 18–28 NCV)

our part

If you've been tracking in our Screw-Ups of the Early Patriarchs series, you will notice that Jacob, who had tricked his brother Esau out of the birthright, is now being duped himself. He loves Rachel. Rachel is the one he wants. He is willing to work for her—and does for seven years, only to be given her older sister (behind a veil) on his wedding night, and he now has to work for seven more years to have Rachel. All of this is extraneous information (but aren't you glad you know [Paul Harvey voiceover] "the rest of the story"?) because the point of this is, when you are truly invested in fully loving someone, matters of time lose relevance. It says that Jacob's seven years of labor went by in a flash because his focus was the end result, not the sacrifice he had to make.

In all marriages, work is required. Lots of work. Years of work. This is the part that many people who are considering marriage don't really get. It's love. It's wonderful. And it's also a lot of work. Like Jacob, you have to take all the work you "think" you will have to do and pretty much double it. That's what it takes.

high note or low note?

Singularity of focus and willingness to earn his bride? High, men. Very high.

your part

Productivity experts and sports analysts call it "the zone"—that state of mind where you lose sense of time and perform at your highest level. You flow and create and accomplish tasks because you are so caught up in the moment. And when you are done, you look at your watch and can't believe the time went by so quickly.

Talk about areas that inspire this sort of "zone" for you. Do you feel that way about the years you have spent together?

your duet

Make a list of things for which you would work fourteen years to obtain. Share your lists with each other. (Hint: Make sure you put your spouse at the top.)

eighteen

The Things We Do for Love

Jacob and Leah
(part two)

listen

Leah became pregnant and gave birth to a son. She named him Reuben, because she said, "The LORD has seen my troubles. Surely now my husband will love me."

Leah became pregnant again and gave birth to another son. She named him Simeon and said, "The

*LORD has heard that I am not loved, so he has given
me this son."*

*Leah became pregnant again and gave birth to
another son. She named him Levi and said, "Now,
surely my husband will be close to me, because I have
given him three sons."*

*Then Leah gave birth to another son. She named
him Judah, because she said, "Now I will praise
the LORD." Then Leah stopped having children.
(Gen. 29:32–35 NCV)*

our part

Wow—this surely is from a soap opera and not the Bible,
right? A woman desperately seeking the love of a man and
deciding that, if the relationship is shaky, a baby will fix it.
And then another, and then another and another.

Look at the kinds of things Leah was seeking (love
and connection). There is nothing wrong with her desires.
But we cannot solidify or correct any relationship deficits
by bringing more people into it. The only thing that

will produce is more damage done to more innocent beings. But not everyone seeks to fix a relationship with pregnancies. Some believe that if they just had more money or status, or if they could just change zip codes, it would fix things—that somehow the answer to their difficulties lies outside of themselves. But contentment and peace and a satisfying relationship with your spouse are things that start internally and work their way out into the space between you. Leah finally came around to the truth that she could just drop her incessant plays for love and attention and just focus on God. What a revelation.

high note or low note?

Right desires—wrong approach. Low.

your part

Have there been times in your relationship when you may have felt that an outward acquisition would solve an inner need? What was the outcome of that experience?

your duet

As much as we would love to be everything to our spouse, there is only One who can be that for us. Ask God to continue to reveal Himself as your ultimate source of love and validation, both as a couple and as individuals.

nineteen

Desperate Measures

Jacob and Rachel
(part three)

listen

When Rachel realized that she wasn't having any children for Jacob, she became jealous of her sister. She told Jacob, "Give me sons or I'll die!"

Jacob got angry with Rachel and said, "Am I God? Am I the one who refused you babies?" (Gen. 30:1–2)

our part

This was not a stellar moment for Jacob or Rachel. She was jealous. She was desperate. She was (dare we say?) hysterical. (By the way, the root of the word *hysterical* comes from the same word as *hysterectomy*, meaning "hormone related"—perhaps not a good point to bring up if a woman is, in fact, feeling hysterical. Nothing makes a woman feel less validated than blaming her behavior on hormones—deserved or not.)

When a woman says, "If _____ doesn't happen, I will die," this is a declaration of the strongest kind, and it carries with it a need for empathy and a skill set that involves much kind reasoning and the ability to talk someone off an emotional ledge. Not to gender-generalize, but this seems to happen more often with one gender than the other. But women do *feel* things deeply. It's part of the way they are hardwired. So—is that gentle, reasoning, talking-down-from-the-ledge approach what happened in this scenario? Decidedly not. Jacob responded in a most recognizable man-speak: "I can't fix this so I'm mad." Sound like anything that has ever transpired between you and your spouse? Jacob is not only angry, but telling

Rachel that her emotions are misplaced—in effect saying, "I'm not God. I'm not the one you should be kvetching at!"

But in marriage we do take out our frustrations on each other. These are not our proudest moments, but we can (as we learn to control the urge to do otherwise) see this as some sort of backhanded compliment. If we thought that our love could not survive this utter baring of the soul, and that we would be rejected for our feelings in the lowest points of our lives, would we risk exposing our deepest thoughts to each other?

high note or low note?

Lots of bitterness spilling on the table—low.

your part

When the moment is heated and the issues are large, the fact that we are on the same team is often obscured. Your mate can appear to be your enemy just by virtue of the fact that their opinion and life experience are different from yours. It helps to remember to touch each other during an argument as a reminder that you are not opposing each other but rather looking for common ground. Holding a hand or a shoulder can soften a difficult moment.

your duet

Do your disagreements occasionally ramp up into a heated exchange? Can you come up with a code word to stop the escalation in midclimb? Something as silly as "dill pickles" could signal to you both that a three-minute time-out could help you return to the issue later with ideas for empathy and solution rather than attacking each other.

twenty

Beautiful Amnesia

Joseph and Asenath

listen

Joseph had two sons born to him before the years of famine came. Asenath, daughter of Potiphera the priest of On, was their mother. Joseph named the firstborn Manasseh (Forget), saying, "God made me forget all my hardships and my parental home." He named his second son Ephraim (Double Prosperity), saying, "God has prospered me in the land of my sorrow." (Gen. 41:50–52)

our part

It's really great when you get to grow up in a home that is caring and supportive and *Leave It to Beaver*–ish, where conflicts are resolved quickly and lovingly, and bluebirds alight on everyone's forearms. This was not the case for many of us. We grew up in broken homes or had broken people at the helm of our homes.

Joseph's life started off well but went askew for many years during one period in a very, very dark way (betrayal, enslavement, prison time). Here was a man who had much to get past and much to try to forget. And he did it. (Check out Genesis 37—41 for Joseph's amazing story.)

Many of us have gotten trapped into thinking that we have to unpeel all the onions in our past in order to truly move on with life. There are just some things that will never be made right on this earth. And, thankfully, the power of a strong, loving family can help us forget ugly memories from the past. This can be a good thing. Joseph even celebrated this portion of his story by giving his sons names that explained how he felt: *happily forgetful* and *grateful*. If you have had a difficult beginning, it is comforting to know that, through your marriage and family, you can have something that induces a bout of "holy amnesia" and replaces bad memories with a brand-new set of good ones.

high note or low note?

High—Joseph chose to embrace and commemorate a new future with his wife and family.

your part

Every new family unit is a chance to start over. It's not as if you can assume a totally new identity and scrub your past from your permanent record, but you do have the opportunity to create a household that reflects your chosen values and experiences. In Joseph's case, he felt such joy that he gave his children names that celebrated this new start. In what ways has your marriage afforded you this benefit?

your duet

Thank God together for the things that He has allowed you to "forget" in light of the joys that this portion of your journey brings to you.

twenty one

Painful Corrections

Moses and Zipporah

listen

Before Moses left Midian, the LORD said to him,
"Return to Egypt, for all those who wanted to kill you
have died."

So Moses took his wife and sons, put them on a
donkey, and headed back to the land of Egypt. In his
hand he carried the staff of God.

*And the L*ORD *told Moses, "When you arrive back in Egypt, go to Pharaoh and perform all the miracles I have empowered you to do. But I will harden his heart so he will refuse to let the people go. Then you will tell him, 'This is what the L*ORD *says: Israel is my firstborn son. I commanded you, "Let my son go, so he can worship me." But since you have refused, I will now kill your firstborn son!'"*

*On the way to Egypt, at a place where Moses and his family had stopped for the night, the L*ORD *confronted him and was about to kill him. But Moses' wife, Zipporah, took a flint knife and circumcised her son. She touched his feet with the foreskin and said, "Now you are a bridegroom of blood to me." (When she said "a bridegroom of blood," she was referring to the circumcision.) After that, the L*ORD *left him alone. (Ex. 4:19–26* NLT*)*

our part

First let's get this out of the way: Why, oh why was God poised to kill the deliverer of His people? Seems that a little theological disagreement between Moses and Zipporah over the ritual of circumcision of their son had caused a major rift between said deliverer and Sovereign God. Interestingly it is Zipporah who realizes what the point of offense is (women usually intuit these things slightly faster than men) and quickly rectifies the issue with an on-the-spot outpatient procedure. (Right now, every male reading this is probably wincing and potentially holding himself in empathy.) Because of Moses and Zipporah's inability to agree on a spiritual practice, Moses' life was almost lost. We sometimes believe that we can have our separate theologies and everything will work out fine in the end, but if you have leadership responsibilities, God is looking for oneness between a husband and wife. Details do matter.

high note or low note?

Mixed bag—low in that they almost blew it, high because she was quick to respond to save her family.

your part

How close or far apart would you say your theology is from your spouse's? Would you say that this matters, or has not yet mattered, in your relationship? How do you decide what your practice will be when your ideas about spiritual issues don't line up?

your duet

Write a short list of any areas where you have significant theological disagreements. Agree to tackle one issue a week to find a place of agreement (just in case God is ready to zap one of you because of it. Apparently, it does happen sometimes ...).

twenty two

Mr. Deborah, I Presume

Lappidoth and Deborah

listen

A prophetess named Deborah, the wife of Lappidoth, was judge of Israel at that time. Deborah would sit under the Palm Tree of Deborah, which was between the cities of Ramah and Bethel, in the mountains of Ephraim. And the people of Israel would come to her to settle their arguments. (Judg. 4:4–5 NCV)

our part

Possibly the first case of a wife being a national-level leader (the only other persons to hold the trifecta of prophet, judge, and military leader were Moses and Samuel), Deborah ran in the highest of circles. She did not have her career/calling because she had married into it; this woman had discernment, courage, and the ability to rule judiciously. And the people of Israel loved her. Long before there was Joan of Arc, there was Deborah of Israel. Which brings us to Lappidoth, or "Mr. Deborah" as he may have been known. What kind of man does well with a wife in the limelight? It's funny that we never ask the reverse—how does a woman deal with a man in the limelight? (And why is the light infused with lime? But we digress....) We wonder about Stedman and how he deals with being Oprah's boyfriend. And what about the Queen of England's Prince Philip? We don't get much story on Lappidoth, so we can't say how he viewed Deborah's success or how he may have supported it. But we do know that it takes a man who has a sense of history and humility and inner confidence to celebrate his wife's successes.

high note or low note?

High. Off-the-charts, role-flipping high.

your part

So, gentleman of the house, (honestly) how would you respond if your wife were suddenly appointed to the offices of Supreme Court Justice, Joint Chief of Staff, *and* the leader of your church denomination *at the same time?* Would you be a Supportive Lappidoth or a Reluctant Lappidoth? For both husband and wife—what would you be willing to do, as life partners, to accommodate each other as you both transition through times of public recognition and anonymity? Which are easier for you to navigate?

your duet

Draw up an "if one of us ever gets famous" plan of action. It would be fun to dream about it and to realize the downsides to fame. How would you protect your family's privacy? What sacrifices would you be willing to make? What are your absolute nonnegotiables?

twenty three

Femme Assassin

Heber and Jael

listen

"May Jael, the wife of Heber the Kenite,
   be blessed above all women who live in tents.
Sisera asked for water,
   but Jael gave him milk.
In a bowl fit for a ruler,
   she brought him cream.

"Jael reached out and took the tent peg.
   Her right hand reached for the workman's hammer.

She hit Sisera! She smashed his head!
   She crushed and pierced the side of his head!
At Jael's feet he sank.
   He fell, and he lay there.
At her feet he sank. He fell.
   Where Sisera sank, there he fell, dead!

"Let all your enemies die this way, Lord!
   But let all the people who love you
   be as strong as the rising sun!"

Then there was peace in the land for forty years.
(Judg. 5:24–27, 31 NCV)

our part

There are odes to famous (and infamous) characters;
there are songs like "Ode to Billie Joe" and poems like
Keats's and Wordsworth's. But they don't normally
involve the superviolent, double-agent elements of the
"Ode to Jael" we just read. Here was a woman who knew
her way around both a ball-peen hammer and a bowl
of cream. God had commanded the Israelites to utterly

destroy their enemies when they came into Canaan, but they didn't quite finish the job. They left a remnant of enemies who came back to haunt them time and time again, causing unending trouble for the Israelites who had to constantly renegotiate terms of peace with them and live with their heathen demands. Jael's husband, Heber, was one of the men who had decided that he would rather live with the problem than eradicate it. But Jael saw her opportunity to end it (at least for her generation) when the fugitive Sisera came looking for shelter within her tent. We don't know if they had perfected the art of "slipping a mickey" into a drink at that time, but she gave him the sleep-inducing warm-milk treatment, provided him a cushy mat and a cozy afghan, and then worked her hammer-and-tent-spike combo move on his head. While we cannot embrace the violence it took to accomplish it, this does show that a woman will do almost anything in order to get a little peace.

high note or low note?

Heber was doing what he thought best to provide for and protect his family. He was a farmer, and he negotiated the best deal he could to keep his family alive. Jael saw a moment of opportunity and took it. She used all the resources she had to bring about an end to fighting for a generation. And, hey—she got her own ode. A pretty high note—if you don't count the whole murder thing.

your part

God calls us into marriage with different lists of strengths and weaknesses. Usually one person in the marriage is a "let's slow down and look at this from all angles" type and the other is more the "let's leap   we can look later" type. Both are necessary to negotiate life successfully. Take a moment and talk about how these basic temperament differences both frustrate you and enhance your life. Relate one instance where your spouse's strength made it possible for something important to be accomplished that you could not have done without them.

your duet

Imagine that you were in Nazi Germany during World War II and you had the opportunity to assassinate Adolf Hitler. Would you have been a Jael? Would you have been willing to take a single life to save millions?

twenty four

Here's How I See It

Manoah and His Wife

listen

Then Manoah took a young goat and a grain offering and offered it on a rock as a sacrifice to the LORD. And as Manoah and his wife watched, the LORD did an amazing thing. As the flames from the altar shot up toward the sky, the angel of the LORD ascended in the fire. When Manoah and his wife saw this, they fell with their faces to the ground.

The angel did not appear again to Manoah and his wife. Manoah finally realized it was the angel of the LORD, and he said to his wife, "We will certainly die, for we have seen God!"

But his wife said, "If the LORD were going to kill us, he wouldn't have accepted our burnt offering and grain offering. He wouldn't have appeared to us and told us this wonderful thing and done these miracles."

When her son was born, she named him Samson. And the LORD blessed him as he grew up. (Judg. 13:19–24 NLT)

our part

It's a wonderful thing that God decided that marriage was a great plan: to take two distinct people with different experiences and viewpoints and join them at the hip for life—brilliant! You know, other than the intense disagreements and baggage that we bring into the relationship, it's wonderful. And there are times that we get a glimpse into a biblical Ralph-and-Alice-Kramden moment when a wife illuminates a situation that seems rather obvious. As they were worshipping together and a miraculous apparition wafted up in the flames, Manoah goes immediately to the worst-case scenario. He jumped straight to the death sentence, "We're gonna die!" And in her best Alice Kramden, Mrs. Manoah pointed out, "That would be pretty unproductive—to receive our offering or give us the good news that we're having a baby boy—right?" And it is in these moments that we realize that our different experiences and viewpoints actually make for a pretty sweet blend.

high note or low note?

They were worshipping together and were helping each other interpret the signs. We give them a 7.5.

your part

Although our diverse past histories predispose us to occasionally believe that the other person may be from another planet, it is good to have another set of eyes on a happening so that we do not interpret everything from a point of fear. Can you describe a time in your marriage when you and your spouse came at a situation from very different vantage points, and the insight from your spouse helped you see things differently?

your duet

Maybe it's been awhile since you thanked God for your mate's very different viewpoints. Now would be a good time to start.

twenty five

De-Lie-Lah

Samson and Delilah

listen

Some time later Samson fell in love with a woman named Delilah, who lived in the valley of Sorek. The rulers of the Philistines went to her and said, "Entice Samson to tell you what makes him so strong and how he can be overpowered and tied up securely. Then each of us will give you 1,100 pieces of silver."

Then Delilah pouted, [saying to Samson,] "How can you tell me, 'I love you,' when you don't share your secrets with me? You've made fun of me three times now, and you still haven't told me what makes you so strong!" She tormented him with her nagging day after day until he was sick to death of it.

Finally, Samson shared his secret with her. "My hair has never been cut," he confessed, "for I was dedicated to God as a Nazirite from birth. If my head were shaved, my strength would leave me, and I would become as weak as anyone else."

Delilah realized he had finally told her the truth, so she sent for the Philistine rulers. "Come back one more time," she said, "for he has finally told me his secret." So the Philistine rulers returned with the money in their hands. (Judg. 16:4–5, 15–18 NLT)

our part

Can't you just hear Tom Jones singing, "Why, why, whyyyyyyyyyyyyyy, Delilah?" (We just lost everyone under the age of forty, but that's okay.) There is some evidence for strong men in politics. Jesse Ventura and

Arnold Schwarzenegger have been state governors, but no one has asked them to lead the nation. Israel, however, had Samson as a judge (ruler), which is ironic since it was his judgment that was perennially impaired. He was a strong man when it came to biceps but had an eye for the pretty women. Samson was not only strong but was also a dedicated man. He was a Nazirite who had taken vows and was set apart for God's use from childhood. It's no surprise to learn that the name *Delilah* means "weak." We don't know if they were actually married to each other, but their relationship was doomed because of the pack of lies and conspiracy and the wearing down of will. The language used to describe their relationship is telling: "entice," "pouted," "made fun of me," "sick to death of it." Sounds fulfilling, right? They spoke of their love for each other when neither had anything approximating selfless love. They used each other: He loved her attention; she used him to increase her bank account. In the end, there was nothing left but treachery and misery and collapse, because a relationship without truth can never stand.

high note or low note?

Low—so low. Lies never build; they always destroy.

your part

Psalm 51:6 (NCV) says, "You want me to be completely truthful, so teach me wisdom."

What is the truth quotient in your marriage? Do you feel that you can be both authentic and truthful at all times without any fear of being misunderstood or ridiculed? Are you a truth teller by habit? Or is it easier to fudge the truth to preserve your sense of independence?

your duet

Pray for the marital environment that encourages integrity and truth telling. Ask God to give you the kind of relationship that, when all is stripped away, has a bedrock of truth at its core.

twenty six

Only Grieving Once

Elimelech and Naomi

listen

Once upon a time—it was back in the days when judges led Israel—there was a famine in the land. A man from Bethlehem in Judah left home to live in the country of Moab, he and his wife and his two sons. The man's name was Elimelech; his wife's name was Naomi; his sons were named Mahlon and Kilion—all Ephrathites from Bethlehem in Judah. They all went to the country of Moab and settled there.

Elimelech died and Naomi was left, she and her
two sons. The sons took Moabite wives; the name of the
first was Orpah, the second Ruth. They lived there in
Moab for the next ten years. But then the two brothers,
Mahlon and Kilion, died. Now the woman was left
without either her young men or her husband.

"The piece of property that belonged to our relative
Elimelech is being sold by his widow Naomi, who just
returned from the country of Moab." (Ruth 1:1–5;
4:3)

A good man leaves an inheritance for his children's
children, but a sinner's wealth is stored up for the
righteous. (Prov. 13:22 NIV)

our part

They say that the only two sure things are death and
taxes. If you stack famine on top of that, the hardship is
unbearable. Here in the United States we have had rare
brushes with times of universal hardship. Back in biblical
times of famine, it was an entire nation struggling for

basic survival. Such was the case with Naomi's family. The principle was, you did whatever was necessary to take care of the family. That's what Elimelech was trying to do when he died in Moab, leaving his two sons to provide for the family—but they sadly met the same fate as their father. That left three "fragile" (as defined by their culture) females to make it on their own with no other kin in a foreign land. Naomi was able to return to her homeland with Ruth because Elimelech had the foresight to purchase property to provide for his family. That left her with options, rather than being sold into slavery. Because Elimelech leveraged his assets during his lifetime, his family was able to continue without him. The proverb above tells us that Elimelech was, indeed, a good man.

high note or low note?

Providing for your family's present needs and secure future are always high on the "good man's" list.

your part

You have a responsibility in life and even in death to make sure your spouse and family are provided for. One thing you don't want for your family is for them to grieve twice—once on your passing and a second time when they realize you have only left them debt. Talk about how your respective families have handled their planning and what your models have been.

your duet

Get out your will (or make plans to start one right now) and make sure things are up to date. You need to decide as a couple what your estate plans are for the provisions of a surviving spouse. Don't leave your affairs in the hands of others to determine how your beloved and family will be treated.

twenty seven

In with the In-Laws

Boaz and Ruth

listen

Boaz married Ruth. She became his wife. Boaz slept with her. By GOD's gracious gift she conceived and had a son.

The town women said to Naomi, "Blessed be GOD! He didn't leave you without family to carry on your life. May this baby grow up to be famous in Israel! He'll make you young again! He'll take care of you in old age. And this daughter-in-law who has brought

*him into the world and loves you so much, why, she's
worth more to you than seven sons!"*

*Naomi took the baby and held him in her arms,
cuddling him, cooing over him, waiting on him hand
and foot.*

*The neighborhood women started calling him
"Naomi's baby boy!" But his real name was Obed.
Obed was the father of Jesse, and Jesse the father of
David. (Ruth 4:13–17)*

our part

When you marry someone, you really do marry the family.

Ruth may have had more stick-to-itiveness than
the other daughter-in-law, and she felt strongly that
her destiny was tied to her decision to stay with Naomi
and embrace her faith. If you get a chance to read the
entire book of Ruth, you will see that her commitment
was without any assurance of survival or prosperity. But
God brings her to the field of Boaz, and through some
amazing ancestral gyrations, he is eligible to become her

husband. Although we cannot relate to this culturally, this willingness of Boaz to become her "kinsman redeemer" was the equivalent of winning the lottery. Boaz also brought honor to Naomi by choosing to provide for her and take her in. So the chatter of the townswomen around Naomi was all about the reversal of fortune and the value of a loyal daughter-in-law, with the ultimate compliment that she was worth more to Naomi "than seven sons." Wouldn't it be wonderful if, by virtue of our honorable character and actions, our in-laws could say the same about us?

high note or low note?

High—Ruth shows that honoring your spouse's parent can lead to a series of unexpected blessings.

your part

How does this principle of "marrying the family" play itself out in your marriage? Just as we cannot choose our family, we always get a mixed package on the in-law side of things. We do, however, get to choose our attitude and response to the family we become a part of when we marry. Are you able to honor your in-laws? How is that accomplished in your families?

your duet

Regardless of what you think of your in-laws, are there ways you can honor them? We are not suggesting that you let them move in with you or that you write them a long love letter, but brainstorm about how you can honor these people who gave your spouse life (and/or a home).

twenty eight

Whatever You Think Is Best

Elkanah and Hannah

listen

And in due time she gave birth to a son. She named him Samuel, for she said, "I asked the LORD for him."

The next year Elkanah and his family went on their annual trip to offer a sacrifice to the LORD. But Hannah did not go. She told her husband, "Wait until the boy is weaned. Then I will take him to the Tabernacle and leave him there with the LORD permanently."

*"Whatever you think is best," Elkanah agreed. "Stay
here for now, and may the LORD help you keep your
promise." So she stayed home and nursed the boy until
he was weaned.*

*When the child was weaned, Hannah took him to
the Tabernacle in Shiloh. They brought along a three-
year-old bull for the sacrifice and a basket of flour and
some wine. After sacrificing the bull, they brought the
boy to Eli. "Sir, do you remember me?" Hannah asked.
"I am the woman who stood here several years ago
praying to the LORD. I asked the LORD to give me this
boy, and he has granted my request. Now I am giving
him to the LORD, and he will belong to the LORD his
whole life." And they worshiped the LORD there. (1
Sam. 1:20–28 NLT)*

our part

Hannah prayed deliriously for a son. She was shameless
in her pursuit of God for offspring, so much so that the
priest (Eli) accused her of public drunkenness. This did
not deter Hannah in the least. She continued asking God

for a son, and "in due time" (who can know how long, or what constitutes "due" time?) she had her long-awaited baby boy, Samuel. It would be difficult enough to give a son back to the service of the Lord if you had many sons, but only one? Some would say it was lunacy. She believed it was an act of worship to the One who had given him to her. In the exchange between Elkanah and Hannah, we observe that Elkanah did not exactly share Hannah's passion for dedicating the child to God's service, but nonetheless did nothing to prevent it. Here we see a great model for giving way to our spouse when they are filled with fervor and we do not disagree with their decision. Elkanah basically said, "Whatever you need to do, I stand beside you" and prayed for her to have the strength to do what she had vowed to do.

If you are parents, you know how difficult it is to really give your children back to the One who gave them to us. We often mouth great platitudes to that effect, but when it comes to relinquishing them fully, we stop short, believing somehow that we can protect them always. Hannah and Elkanah realized that their child was a temporary blessing who belonged always to God alone.

high note or low note?

High—couples who realize all their blessings are temporary will hold them lightly and each other tightly.

your part

Are there areas of your spouse's walk with God that you just don't quite understand but you encourage them to pursue anyway? Are there some areas that need to move into this category?

your duet

Pray for your partner's spiritual health and release them to follow God in areas that are important to them.

twenty nine

Well-Placed Loyalty

David and Michal

listen

Now Saul's other daughter, Michal, loved David. When they told Saul, he was pleased. He thought, "I will let her marry David. Then she will be a trap for him, and the Philistines will defeat him." So Saul said to David a second time, "You may become my son-in-law."

Saul saw that the LORD was with David and that his daughter Michal loved David. So he grew even more afraid of David, and he was David's enemy all his life. (1 Sam. 18:20–21, 28–29 NCV)

our part

Here is the flip side of the Boaz and Ruth story in chapter 27, where marrying into your spouse's family is a good thing.

Jealousy can make people crazy. There's a reason the words *insanely* and *jealous* are often paired up. Those who are jealous are particularly dangerous if they are in a position of power and are family by marriage.

We're fairly certain that none of you reading this book has a father-in-law with a price on your head. Such was the plight of David and Michal. It speaks to the depravity of Saul that he was pleased to hear of Michal's love for David because it fit his Machiavellian scheme to keep his friends close and his enemies closer. But Saul seriously underestimated the loyalty of Michal to her husband. She took the "leave and cleave" principle seriously and rightly prioritized her commitments. In 1 Samuel 19, Michal helps David escape Saul's murderous plots and thus incurs her father's wrath. Her commitment to David did not waver. Her love for him superseded her commitment to her family of origin, which is as it should be. For some who are reading this, the in-law may not be psychotic nor the situation as dangerous, but the issue is still the same: Whose family are you in?

high note or low note?

This is a high note, because Michal committed fully to her husband, and the trust factor between the two was strong.

your part

Are you ever tempted to discuss your spouse with your parents or your in-laws? As much as they may love you, the new family unit does not need to share everything with the old family unit. They may be well intentioned, but everyone can slip into a "knowledge is power" mind-set if the wrong situation presents itself. Have there been times when you wished that you had not revealed information, and it came back to haunt you? There is a freedom in living transparently, but we must be wise with what we choose to share.

your duet

Many couples are willing to die for each other, but the question is, *Will you live for each other?* Because of your love and commitment for your spouse, list one thing that you would be willing to do for them starting right now.

thirty

Peace Offerings

Nabal and Abigail

listen

There was a wealthy man from Maon who owned property near the town of Carmel. He had 3,000 sheep and 1,000 goats, and it was sheep-shearing time. This man's name was Nabal, and his wife, Abigail, was a sensible and beautiful woman. But Nabal, a descendant of Caleb, was crude and mean in all his dealings.

Meanwhile, one of Nabal's servants went to Abigail and told her, "David sent messengers from the

*wilderness to greet our master, but he screamed insults
at them. These men have been very good to us, and
we never suffered any harm from them. Nothing was
stolen from us the whole time they were with us. In
fact, day and night they were like a wall of protection
to us and the sheep. You need to know this and figure
out what to do, for there is going to be trouble for our
master and his whole family. He's so ill-tempered that
no one can even talk to him!"*

*Abigail wasted no time. She quickly gathered 200
loaves of bread, two wineskins full of wine, five sheep
that had been slaughtered, nearly a bushel of roasted
grain, 100 clusters of raisins, and 200 fig cakes. She
packed them on donkeys and said to her servants, "Go
on ahead. I will follow you shortly." But she didn't tell
her husband Nabal what she was doing.*

*As she was riding her donkey into a mountain
ravine, she saw David and his men coming toward
her. David had just been saying, "A lot of good it
did to help this fellow. We protected his flocks in the*

wilderness, and nothing he owned was lost or stolen.
But he has repaid me evil for good. May God strike me
and kill me if even one man of his household is still
alive tomorrow morning!"

When Abigail saw David, she quickly got off her
donkey and bowed low before him. She fell at his feet
and said, "I accept all blame in this matter, my lord.
Please listen to what I have to say. I know Nabal is
a wicked and ill-tempered man; please don't pay any
attention to him. He is a fool, just as his name suggests.
But I never even saw the young men you sent.

"Now, my lord, as surely as the LORD lives and
you yourself live, since the LORD has kept you from
murdering and taking vengeance into your own hands,
let all your enemies and those who try to harm you be
as cursed as Nabal is. And here is a present that I, your
servant, have brought to you and your young men."
(1 Sam. 25:2–3, 14–27 NLT)

our part

One of the unspoken agreements of marriage (which possibly should be in the marriage vows) is that each of the partners will have to pick up the slack for the other from time to time. We all have blind spots. We will all play the part of a fool now and then. Hopefully, none of us will have the description "foolishness oozes from him" as Nabal did. But we all occasionally do foolish things for which our more socially aware spouse will have to come behind and make amends, patch things up, smooth things over. Some may tag Abigail as the codependent enabler of a drunkard. But Abigail had the smarts to see a storm coming with David's crew, and she intercepted with an offering of humility and carbs. And because of it, her household was spared. In an interesting twist (if you read further in the passage), her brute of a husband has a heart attack and dies, and Abigail becomes David's wife. No doubt because she had a cool head and made a mean fig cake.

high note or low note?

Married to a fool is unfortunate. Able to compensate for your spouse's weaknesses is sometimes grace in action.

your part

This is a good time to acknowledge that we all need an assist now and again. It is God's grace in our lives if we have someone who always has our backs and will step up to head off disaster when we cannot see that our ways are going to cost us something we are not prepared to pay. These graces are part of the cement of our history together. We may be blessed to have a partner who loves us enough to stick with us despite our faults, and who offers their strengths to offset them.

your duet

Each of you, take a piece of paper and list your various strengths and weakness (*yours,* not your spouse's). Look at how there are many areas where you are polar opposites in your list. Your weaknesses may be some of your spouse's strengths. Although this seems maddening at times, celebrate how each of you challenges the other to be more well rounded.

thirty one

Power Tripped

Ahab and Jezebel

listen

*Ahab son of Omri became king of Israel in the
thirty-eighth year of Asa king of Judah. Ahab son of
Omri was king over Israel for twenty-two years. He
ruled from Samaria. Ahab son of Omri did even
more open evil before G*OD *than anyone yet—a new
champion in evil! It wasn't enough for him to copy the
sins of Jeroboam son of Nebat; no, he went all out, first
by marrying Jezebel daughter of Ethbaal king of the
Sidonians, and then by serving and worshiping the god*

*Baal. He built a temple for Baal in Samaria, and then
furnished it with an altar for Baal. Worse, he went
on and built a shrine to the sacred whore Asherah. He
made the GOD of Israel angrier than all the previous
kings of Israel put together.*

*When Jezebel heard that Jehu had arrived in Jezreel,
she made herself up—put on eyeshadow and arranged
her hair—and posed seductively at the window. When
Jehu came through the city gate, she called down, "So,
how are things, 'Zimri,' you dashing king-killer?"*

*Jehu looked up at the window and called, "Is there
anybody up there on my side?" Two or three palace
eunuchs looked out.*

*He ordered, "Throw her down!" They threw her
out the window. Her blood spattered the wall and the
horses, and Jehu trampled her under his horse's hooves.*

*Then Jehu went inside and ate his lunch. During
lunch he gave orders, "Take care of that damned*

woman; give her a decent burial—she is, after all, a king's daughter."

They went out to bury her, but there was nothing left of her but skull, feet, and hands. They came back and told Jehu. He said, "It's GOD's word, the word spoken by Elijah the Tishbite:
In the field of Jezreel,
dogs will eat Jezebel;

The body of Jezebel will be like
dog-droppings on the ground in Jezreel.
Old friends and lovers will say,
'I wonder, is this Jezebel?'" (1 Kings 16:29–33;
2 Kings 9:30–37)

our part

Jezebel—you were one evil woman. So much so that you ended up as dog dung, an archetype, and a punch line. Along the way you killed a lot of good people and incited your husband to his lowest possible deeds. You practically invented the phrase "the end justifies the means." And you thought you got away with most of it.

This is a story of a couple who would have been mean and vicious separately. But when you combined their worst traits together, they became a power couple to be feared. They were Baal worshippers, and their blatant idol temples fired up God's wrath-o-meter way past the red zone. She was a seductress and lived by her own impulses. And we all know that we are capable of encouraging each other's worst traits at times. But you can't remain on this kind of power trip forever; comeuppance does come. She may have lived high on the hog for a while, but every dog has its day.

high note or low note?
Limbo, limbo, limbo. How low can you go?

your part
We can all drift toward our lower nature from time to time. How do we stake ourselves to biblical truth to stop the drift? What are you doing as a couple (aside from reading this book) to ensure that God's Word is an integral

part of your life so that it will guide you in your everyday decision-making processes? Discuss what you want your children and grandchildren to remember about your life.

your duet

Ask God to remind you of the good traits of your spouse and to realize that a good spouse is truly a gift from God.

thirty two

Legislate It

King Xerxes and Queen Vashti

listen

This is the story of something that happened in the time of Xerxes, the Xerxes who ruled from India to Ethiopia—127 provinces in all. King Xerxes ruled from his royal throne in the palace complex of Susa. In the third year of his reign he gave a banquet for all his officials and ministers. The military brass of Persia and Media were also there, along with the princes and governors of the provinces.

The guests could drink as much as they liked—
king's orders!—with waiters at their elbows to refill
the drinks. Meanwhile, Queen Vashti was throwing
a separate party for women inside King Xerxes' royal
palace.

On the seventh day of the party, the king, high
on the wine, ordered the seven eunuchs who were
his personal servants (Mehuman, Biztha, Harbona,
Bigtha, Abagtha, Zethar, and Carcas) to bring
him Queen Vashti resplendent in her royal crown.
He wanted to show off her beauty to the guests and
officials. She was extremely good-looking.

But Queen Vashti refused to come, refused the
summons delivered by the eunuchs. The king lost
his temper. Seething with anger over her insolence,
the king called in his counselors, all experts in legal
matters. It was the king's practice to consult his expert
advisors. Those closest to him were Carshena, Shethar,
Admatha, Tarshish, Meres, Marsena, and Memucan,
the seven highest-ranking princes of Persia and Media,

the inner circle with access to the king's ear. He asked
them what legal recourse they had against Queen
Vashti for not obeying King Xerxes' summons delivered
by the eunuchs.

"So, if the king agrees, let him pronounce a royal
ruling and have it recorded in the laws of the Persians
and Medes so that it cannot be revoked, that Vashti is
permanently banned from King Xerxes' presence. And
then let the king give her royal position to a woman
who knows her place. When the king's ruling becomes
public knowledge throughout the kingdom, extensive
as it is, every woman, regardless of her social position,
will show proper respect to her husband." (Est. 1:1–3,
9–15, 19–20)

our part

If only the World Health Organization would move
so swiftly and decisively to head off the spread of new
contagions! Xerxes (the original "X" Man) was a very,
very powerful man. As such, he was used to people doing
his bidding without question or hesitation. I'm sure that

when he married his queen, Vashti, her free spirit and refusal to be bound by convention captivated him. This is all well and good until you need Ms. Free-to-Be-Me to make an appearance at your state dinner. Vashti was elsewhere having a girls' getaway weekend. Never mind that Xerxes was objectifying her, he wanted to show her off. She flatout refused the man. It's not clear if she believed that she could get away with this or if she was so o-v-e-r it, but it *is* clear that she did not cotton to his desire. He objectified her; she defied him. His temper was riled; she got the boot (this often happens when one marries an absolute ruler).

But the last sentence of this passage shows that Xerxes was more interested in making an example of her than resolving their issues. His plan was that, because of her rejection and humiliation, all women of all social stations would forever and always respect their men. (Oh, by the way, King X, your plan hasn't really had the desired effect throughout the ages....)

high note or low note?

Another tale of two very human humans, acting out of ego, tossing out the relationship for trumped-up "principles." Low.

your part

Ephesians 5:33 lets us know that love from a husband and respect from a wife are primary needs in any marriage. When both partners are freely giving (regardless of whether we understand *why* they need it, they just *do*) it creates a positive, honoring environment in which love can flourish. When one partner withholds these needs from the other, it becomes a downward spiral that brings with it anger and acrimony.

What are the patterns in your family of origin that you observed in your formative years? How have these molded you (positively or negatively) in your marriage today?

your duet

Wives, ask your husbands to complete this sentence:
"I feel respected most whenever you _____
_____."

Husbands, ask your wives to complete this sentence:
"I feel loved most whenever you _____

_____
_____."

thirty three

Your Wish Is My Command

Xerxes and Esther

listen

On the third day of the fast, Esther put on her royal robes and entered the inner court of the palace, just across from the king's hall. The king was sitting on his royal throne, facing the entrance. When he saw Queen Esther standing there in the inner court, he welcomed her and held out the gold scepter to her. So Esther approached and touched the end of the scepter.

Then the king asked her, "What do you want, Queen Esther? What is your request? I will give it to you, even if it is half the kingdom!"

And Esther replied, "If it please the king, let the king and Haman come today to a banquet I have prepared for the king."

The king turned to his attendants and said, "Tell Haman to come quickly to a banquet, as Esther has requested." So the king and Haman went to Esther's banquet.

And while they were drinking wine, the king said to Esther, "Now tell me what you really want. What is your request? I will give it to you, even if it is half the kingdom!"

Esther replied, "This is my request and deepest wish. If I have found favor with the king, and if it pleases the king to grant my request and do what I ask, please come with Haman tomorrow to the banquet I will prepare for you. Then I will explain what this is all about." (Est. 5:1–8 NLT)

our part

Use the force, Luke.

It makes sense in *Star Wars,* and it makes sense in the story of Esther.

Esther followed a queen (Vashti) who inflamed the anger of her king and, as the replacement queen, she knew that you catch a lot more flies with honey than vinegar. Esther's interest in pleasing the king was not for her own power or to engage in vain manipulation, but she knew that God had ordained their union to save her people. But beyond her purpose, Esther reveals a wonderful truth: If we spend our time and energies planning things that bless our spouse, there is literally nothing they will not do to bless us in return. The problem is that our culture has taught us quite the opposite—that we must look after our own interests and grab everything we can for ourselves. That mentality makes us narcissistic and empty, because we were not designed to attain fulfillment in that manner. When we are followers of Christ, we are instructed to honor each other, esteem each other, and attend to each other's needs before consideration of our own. Esther stands as a testimony to the power of blessing your spouse. May the force be with you.

high note or low note?

Esther knew the power of giving. She created an upward spiral of blessing one another.

your part

So many of us wait for our partner to be the one to initiate or start something good. How different could our marriages be if we did not wait to be acted upon, but appointed ourselves the task of seeking out ways to bless our spouse and then watch the positive vortex begin to reel us in? Does your day begin with your mental list of needs, or does it begin with a list of ways to make life better for the one whom you love?

your duet

Well, now that you both know that this is a powerful principle, it will be interesting to see who can out-bless the other this week. Maybe it's an area where you can be über-competitive and everyone wins. Find a way to bless your mate before sunrise tomorrow.

thirty four

Harsh Words in Hard Times

Job and Job's Wife

listen

> So Satan went forth from the presence of the Lord
> and smote Job with loathsome and painful sores from
> the sole of his foot to the crown of his head.
>
> And he took a piece of broken pottery with which to
> scrape himself, and he sat [down] among the ashes.
>
> Then his wife said to him, Do you still hold fast
> your blameless uprightness? Renounce God and die!

But he said to her, You speak as one of the impious and foolish women would speak. What? Shall we accept [only] good at the hand of God and shall we not accept [also] misfortune and what is of a bad nature? In [spite of] all this, Job did not sin with his lips. (Job 2:7–10 AB)

our part

Talk about kicking a man when he's down....

Mrs. Job did not come with much of an empathy gene, did she? It might be easy to dismiss her question with the idea that she was heartless, but she had also lost her ten children, her home, her financial security—and, though she was not in the same physical shape as Job, she had plenty of reason to be bitter. So when she asks her husband if he was still clinging to a God who had brought him all this pain, she probably said it with less of the sneer we infer and perhaps more of the vacant look of a woman who feels God-forsaken and scared. It's hard to be encouraging when you can't see a ray of hope yourself. But in every couple there is usually one who continues to hope against all odds and one who can hardly see hope when it's standing right in front of them. It's another of those strength/weakness dynamics that makes marriage the mystery that it is. Job reminded her that the same God who allowed the devastation had given them the blessings to begin with. And although Job did question God about what had happened, he did not question God's right to do with whomever whatever He wished.

high note or low note?

Mrs. Job's jib-jab: low. The fact that Job did not kick her to the curb for it: high.

Fortunate for Mrs. Job, he was in no condition to kick anyone anywhere.

your part

Write it down: *"There will be trouble in my life."* This is not because we wish it on you. Jesus promised that it would happen: "In this world you will have trouble" (John 16:33 NIV), but He *also* promised that He has overcome this. Unfortunately we assume that means we will be immediately delivered from the trouble not long after it starts, which is *not* promised. The question, then, is how will we deal with the trouble when it comes? Which one of you is perennially hope filled? And does the other claim to be "more of a realist" (code words for "hardly ever hope filled")? Perhaps this might be a good time to make a pact to skip the Mrs. Job approach should you ever suffer an enormous loss.

your duet

Ask God to protect your marriage and family. Also ask Him to help you. When trials come, place your faith squarely where it belongs (in the God who loves you), and preserve your relationships when the going gets rough. Praying this in times of blessing helps you remember it in times of trouble.

thirty five

Let Me Stalk You a Little
(In a Good Way)

Solomon and His Beloved
(part one)

listen

Tell me where you're working
   —I love you so much—
Tell me where you're tending your flocks,
   where you let them rest at noontime.
Why should I be the one left out,
   outside the orbit of your tender care? (Song 1:7)

our part

So when was the last time you asked your partner to let you come to where he or she works around lunchtime and just hang out because you needed a little TLC? Not lately? Us either. But what a great way to express your desire to be with your love, even though you understand that they have a real job with real responsibilities. Proximity has its privileges. Our little dog, Maggie, will just jump up in the middle of the sofa and virtually demand a little attention whenever she feels she needs it. She doesn't wait for an invitation; she just knows that if there is attention to be given, she will make herself available to get some. It seems like that is what Solomon's beloved is saying: Why do your flocks get all your love and attention when I need some of that? And wouldn't it be great to consider all of the stuff that happens when you're apart to be just a series of interruptions until you can resume what you really consider important—loving your beloved?

high note or low note?

This is a woman who knows how to make herself available to receive the love she needs. High.

your part

Are you good at expressing to your partner when your love tank feels a little empty? Do you feel that you can ask for attention when you feel it is lacking, or do you wait for your beloved to notice that something is wrong? We have learned that we need to ask for what we need because—though it may seem less romantic—it is actually more romantic to trust that your partner is eager to please you and love you in ways they may not have known you needed. Plus it saves a *lot* of time.

your duet

Take this moment to practice asking for something from your partner (a display of affection, eye contact, more time together in the afternoons—whatever you really need from them), and trust that your lover wants to give you the love you need.

thirty six

When You Care Enough to Give a Little Somethin'

Solomon and His Beloved
(part two)

listen

> *You remind me of Pharaoh's*
> *well-groomed and satiny mares.*

> *Pendant earrings line the elegance of your cheeks;*
> *strands of jewels illumine the curve of your*
> *throat.*

> *I'm making jewelry for you, gold and silver jewelry*
> *that will mark and accent your beauty.*
> *(Song 1:9-11)*

our part

What is it about little gifts? It can't be the gift itself, because sometimes they are small and inexpensive. Is it what it conveys about the recipient? Or is it just the idea that someone took the time to think about us? All of those could be true, but the core issue is that love gives. It's one of the central themes of 1 Corinthians 13 and the motivating factor behind God the Father sending Jesus to earth: Love gives. When we truly love someone, there is a delight in surprising them and showering them with tokens that say, "I love you and this made me think of you and I can't wait to give this to you." It could be something as simple as a silly sticker (with a funny phrase that made you think of them) or an elaborate, expensive gift (nice if you've got the disposable income as Solomon did). But even with his unlimited resources, the passage above tells us that Solomon was "making jewelry" for her. Whether he was commissioning it or hammering out the silver himself, the bottom line is that he was personally involved in creating something special for her. And whether it's a picked-straight-from-the-flower-bed stem or a box from Tiffany's, nothing warms a girl's heart like a thought that turns into an action.

high note or low note?
The man is just a love machine. High note after high note. Put him in the Love Hall of Fame.

your part
There are moments that stand out in a day. Any moment that you are the recipient of an unexpected, spontaneous gift that comes from a heart of love is a standout moment. Talk about some of your memories of moments like that in your relationship.

your duet
The best gift givers pay attention. Start a "love gives" list (on some paper, in a folder on your computer—wherever you can drop ideas in to fish from later), and look for opportunities to surprise one another with a thought that counts.

thirty seven

Lovesick

Solomon and His Beloved
(part three)

listen

[She said] I am only a little rose or autumn crocus of the plain of Sharon, or a [humble] lily of the valleys [that grows in deep and difficult places].

But Solomon replied, Like the lily among thorns, so are you, my love, among the daughters.

Like an apple tree among the trees of the wood, so is
my beloved [shepherd] among the sons [cried the girl]!
Under his shadow I delighted to sit, and his fruit was
sweet to my taste.

He brought me to the banqueting house, and
his banner over me was love [for love waved as a
protecting and comforting banner over my head when
I was near him].

Sustain me with raisins, refresh me with apples, for
I am sick with love. (Song 2:1–5 AB)

our part

Do you remember (try to access this feeling now … you may have to reach back a little, but we're sure it's there somewhere) when you were first in love and your stomach did little flips when you *merely anticipated* being with your love, not to mention when you were actually in their presence? C'mon—it happened, right? You didn't even want to eat because you were all atwitter with just the thought of being with the one you loved. It was a real sensation in the pit of your stomach. Such jittery, nervous energy. It was so consuming. You doodled their name on your notebook, you daydreamed about what you would say the next time you were together. And when you think about it now, you cannot begin to explain how that amount of captivation could have hijacked your frontal lobe for that amount of time. It was a serious case of lovesickness. And it's time to bring it back! Yes, you can (even after years of lunches and mortgages and disagreements and kids and in-laws and yard work and taxes and bills and laundry)! What we learn from this Lover Man and his Lover Woman is that love takes attention. *Whatever you make the object of your attention will bring you this sort of distraction.* And really, couldn't the world use a few lovesick lunatics to inspire us all?

high note or low note?

Driven to distraction, lovesick and proud of it: highest.

your part

Let's take a stroll down memory lane and access that first blush of love and recall the crazy/stupid/illogical things you did as a result of your lovesick status with your spouse. Take a moment to talk about things you can do to cut through the clutter in your life and refocus your attention on the person to whom you have committed your life.

your duet

A little nostalgia never hurt anybody. Make a date to re-create one of your first (or favorite) dating experiences. Do you need to travel somewhere to make it happen? Do it!

thirty eight

Trysting

Solomon and His Beloved
(part four)

listen

[So I went with him, and when we were climbing the rocky steps up the hillside, my beloved shepherd said to me] O my dove, [while you are here] in the seclusion of the clefts in the solid rock, in the sheltered and secret place of the cliff, let me see your face, let me hear your voice; for your voice is sweet, and your face is lovely. (Song 2:14 AB)

our part

Behold the power of the tryst. (Doesn't it just sound sexy?) There is no denying that this couple knew how to keep the love red hot and happening. They would slip away into the "seclusion of the clefts" and steal some serious face time with each other. Nothing makes you feel more dangerous than when you're taking love when it is unexpected. It is a shame that some Christians have been brainwashed to believe that monogamous, godly love is somehow supposed to be bland and predictable and—let's face it—boring. We believe that this notion is best expressed in the theological term *baloney*. God invented sex and the pleasure that our bodies feel when we are engaged in it. How in the world we let the culture hijack that into a marketing tool and lead us to believe that we are somehow "less than" when we enjoy it in the confines of a committed *married* relationship is nothing short of a tragedy. If you read the account of Adam and Eve in Genesis and see that the man and the woman were created to enjoy each other, you can't deny that the pleasure we seek with each other through sex is one of God's best ideas. Ever.

high note or low note?
Hot, hot, and did we mention hot?

your part
Have you perhaps, uh … misplaced your desire for your lover? Are you a little less likely to be looking for a tryst than for your socks or the kids' lunch money? If your last memory of a romantic tryst with your beloved is accompanied with music from another decade, it's time to get back to the kind of stuff that got you guys in deep in the beginning.

your duet
So this seems obvious, but wouldn't it just ramp up the anticipation in your relationship if both of you agreed to plan some sort of surprise tryst with each other in the next thirty days? And then you actually followed through with it? Prepare for some exciting, secretive love!

thirty nine

In Over My Head

Solomon and His Beloved
(part five)

listen

Dear, dear friend and lover,
   you're as beautiful as Tirzah, city of delights,
Lovely as Jerusalem, city of dreams,
   the ravishing visions of my ecstasy.
Your beauty is too much for me—I'm in over my head.
   I'm not used to this! I can't take it in.

Your hair flows and shimmers
*   like a flock of goats in the distance*
*   streaming down a hillside in the sunshine.*
Your smile is generous and full—
*   expressive and strong and clean.*
Your veiled cheeks
*   are soft and radiant.*

There's no one like her on earth,
*   never has been, never will be.*
She's a woman beyond compare.
*   My dove is perfection,*
Pure and innocent as the day she was born,
*   and cradled in joy by her mother.*
Everyone who came by to see her
*   exclaimed and admired her—*
All the fathers and mothers, the neighbors and friends,
*   blessed and praised her:*

"Has anyone ever seen anything like this—
*   dawn-fresh, moon-lovely, sun-radiant,*

ravishing as the night sky with its galaxies of stars?" (Song 6:4–10)

our part

In the middle of this recitation of his beloved's various attributes (and admit it—the man does know how to craft a compliment), Solomon states that he is in over his head. Every man knows the meaning of "out-punting your coverage," but Solomon is saying that trying to take his beloved in is like trying to take a drink from a fire hydrant, and he is virtually drowning in an ocean of love. That he is willing to admit his awestruck-ness in the face of such beauty and his powerlessness to control what he feels in response to it is remarkable because he is a most powerful ruler. It would seem that this would make him reluctant to admit anything and keep his cards close to the vest—but he does the exact opposite. This man is not too cool and controlling to express himself, he is just frustrated that his impressive vocabulary still does not afford him enough words to get the job done properly. He sings along with John Denver, "Let me drown in your laughter, let me die in your arms."

high note or low note?

Seriously … is this even a question?

your part

Expression of love is like the flower on the plant. The plant may be alive and functioning and healthy, but the flower makes it beautiful. When we love and do not give expression to it, we are denying ourselves the most beautiful parts of our love. It takes thought and attention to find words to express how you feel about your spouse, but it's definitely worth the effort. Take a moment to talk about why you may feel reluctant to express yourself verbally with your mate.

your duet

Write a Solomon-ish love letter to your beloved.

Make a date to meet in the bathtub to read them to each other. Soon.

When You Sum It All Up

Zachariah and Elizabeth
(part one)

listen

*During the rule of Herod, King of Judea, there was
a priest assigned service in the regiment of Abijah. His
name was Zachariah. His wife was descended from the
daughters of Aaron. Her name was Elizabeth. Together
they lived honorably before God, careful in keeping to
the ways of the commandments and enjoying a clear
conscience before God. (Luke 1:5–6)*

our part

It kinda makes you wonder what your marriage's three-phrase summation would be if you were included in the Bible, doesn't it? Would it be "lived slightly above their means, had a date night every Thursday, and enjoyed an occasional season of feeling closer to God every now and then"? For Zachariah and Elizabeth, their three-phrase description boils it down to the health of their spiritual life: They were honorable, commandment-keeping people who had no trouble living with their choices. Is there a greater compliment paid to a marriage in all of Scripture? They saw their life as being played out to an audience of One, and it was obviously clear to those around them that they valued His opinion more than anyone else's. The Scripture also tells us that they were "careful in keeping" commandments, implying that they were not just interested in the showy broad strokes, but attentive to the details and faithful in the small things. The result of a lifetime of daily right choices and a long obedience over time is a clear conscience before God. Peace. Couldn't every marriage use a truckload of that?

high note or low note?
A high compliment to any couple.

your part
How do you feel your marriage is holding up under the Zach/Liz model? Are you honorable? Obedient? Do you have a clear conscience as a couple? Is there peace between each other and with God?

your duet
Take out a piece of paper for each of you. In sixty seconds or less, write out your three-phrase summary of your marriage in its current state. Compare them. Then write (together) what you want your three-phrase summary of your marriage to be when remembered generations from now.

forty one

I Seriously Doubt It

Zachariah and Elizabeth
(part two)

listen

Zachariah said to the angel, "Do you expect me to believe this? I'm an old man and my wife is an old woman."

But the angel said, "I am Gabriel, the sentinel of God, sent especially to bring you this glad news. But because you won't believe me, you'll be unable to say a word until the day of your son's birth. Every word I've spoken to you will come true on time—God's time."

Meanwhile, the congregation waiting for Zachariah was getting restless, wondering what was keeping him so long in the sanctuary. When he came out and couldn't speak, they knew he had seen a vision. He continued speechless and had to use sign language with the people.

When Elizabeth was full-term in her pregnancy, she bore a son. Her neighbors and relatives, seeing that God had overwhelmed her with mercy, celebrated with her.

On the eighth day, they came to circumcise the child and were calling him Zachariah after his father. But his mother intervened: "No. He is to be called John."

"But," they said, "no one in your family is named that." They used sign language to ask Zachariah what he wanted him named.

*Asking for a tablet, Zachariah wrote, "His name is
to be John." That took everyone by surprise. Surprise
followed surprise—Zachariah's mouth was now open,
his tongue loose, and he was talking, praising God!*

*A deep, reverential fear settled over the
neighborhood, and in all that Judean hill country
people talked about nothing else. Everyone who heard
about it took it to heart, wondering, "What will
become of this child? Clearly, God has his hand in
this." (Luke 1:18–22, 57–66)*

our part

Having spent years in Christian ministry, we can attest
that there are expectations that come with the office.
People think that you are somehow more spiritual than
they are, that maybe you quote Scripture while you stir
your coffee or maybe you don't wrestle with doubt the way
they do. Zachariah found himself standing squarely in a
sea of doubt while performing his sacrifice of faith. While
his congregation awaited his return from the Holy Place,
he was in there arguing with an angel. Not exactly priestly

activities. Reminiscent of Abraham and Sarah's exchange, Zachariah just could not bring himself to believe that he and his (heretofore) barren wife were to have a son. He was dumbstruck, literally. And that's what happens to all of us in our moments of doubt; we lose our "voice"—our ability to speak life into situations. Doubt carries with it no gifts. We lose heart and faith. We dwell in a world where the only sure thing is hard and fast proof. So Zachariah was left to observe in silence throughout the miraculous pregnancy followed by a miraculous birth. He could not express his joy in fatherhood or his gratitude to God. How frustrating that must've been for him and for Elizabeth. She could not hear her husband affirm her and celebrate with her. He was there, but was a silent partner—until he was asked to confirm the name of the child. Little wonder that when his voice was restored, his first use of it was to praise God. And we bet he never stopped.

high note or low note?

Both—doubt can paralyze us even in miraculous moments. It is a blessing when both partners don't doubt simultaneously.

your part

There are moments (months? years?) in most marriages when it seems like your spouse "goes silent" for a while. This can be due to doubt, depression, illness, or difficulty dealing with setbacks. How have you come through these times together? If you have not experienced one of these yet, how can you build things into your marriage now that will carry you through the "silent" times?

your duet

In John 20, doubting Thomas eventually believed that Jesus was the Savior. Pray that the Lord would shore up the areas in your life that are riddled with doubt and that you will be able to speak life into your marriage and family because your faith remains strong.

forty two

A Circle of Trust

Joseph and Mary
(part one)

listen

The birth of Jesus took place like this. His mother, Mary, was engaged to be married to Joseph. Before they came to the marriage bed, Joseph discovered she was pregnant. (It was by the Holy Spirit, but he didn't know that.) Joseph, chagrined but noble, determined to take care of things quietly so Mary would not be disgraced.

*While he was trying to figure a way out, he had a
dream. God's angel spoke in the dream: "Joseph, son of
David, don't hesitate to get married. Mary's pregnancy
is Spirit-conceived. God's Holy Spirit has made her
pregnant. She will bring a son to birth, and when she
does, you, Joseph, will name him Jesus—'God saves'—
because he will save his people from their sins." This
would bring the prophet's embryonic sermon to full term:*

> *Watch for this—a virgin will get pregnant
>   and bear a son;
> They will name him Immanuel
>   (Hebrew for "God is with us").*

*Then Joseph woke up. He did exactly what God's
angel commanded in the dream: He married Mary.
But he did not consummate the marriage until she had
the baby. He named the baby Jesus. (Matt. 1:18–25)*

our part

It was all a matter of trust. Mary could be trusted with the
baby. Joseph could be trusted with Mary (not to have her

stoned or abandon her). The message the angel brought in the dream could be trusted because it was from God. Joseph could be trusted to act on the message of the dream. The level of trust that was required from all parties involved was enormous. For two very young people this was a lot to handle. It's as if they were thrown into the deep end of the trust pool and they had to swim. It is a good thing they had a message from an angel to buoy them. There was no way they were going to win in the court of public opinion. There would always be whispers that they had not honored the bounds of betrothal. Or that Mary had stepped out on Joseph. But Joseph and Mary knew what they knew. They shared knowledge of something supernatural that bound them together beyond mere promises. It was all a matter of trust.

high note or low note?

Very high. Very deep. Trust taken to an exponential level.

your part

In the movie *Meet the Parents,* Robert De Niro's character talks about their family's "circle of trust" and explains that people cannot just enter into it without proving themselves. Discuss the events in your marriage that have proven that the "circle of trust" between you is strong. Do you think God could trust you with the kind of experience Mary and Joseph had? It will never happen again, but do you think you would have been able to see it through had it been you?

your duet

Ask God to increase your capacity for trust in the heart of your spouse and to make you more trustworthy.

forty three

Taxing Affairs

Joseph and Mary
(part two)

listen

Now in those days a decree went out from Caesar Augustus, that a census be taken of all the inhabited earth. This was the first census taken while Quirinius was governor of Syria. And everyone was on his way to register for the census, each to his own city. Joseph also went up from Galilee, from the city of Nazareth, to Judea, to the city of David which is called Bethlehem, because he was of the house and family of David, in order to register along with Mary, who was engaged to him, and was with child.

While they were there, the days were completed for her to give birth.

And she gave birth to her firstborn son; and she wrapped Him in cloths, and laid Him in a manger, because there was no room for them in the inn. (Luke 2:1–7 NASB)

our part

Taxes, taxes, taxes. The more things change, the more they stay the same. Why is it that the government doesn't care if you are inconvenienced by their rules about times and seasons and places and taxes? It's not like Joseph and Mary could just file electronically or stick the form in an envelope and mail it in. No, they had to go there—and it was a decree. So Joseph and Mary had to make their way to Bethlehem and, though the images on the Christmas cards would lead you to believe that there was a ride on a gentle donkey involved, that is just artistic license. More likely than not, it was a long walk with a very pregnant fiancée. Even if it was a donkey ride, have you ever taken one? Not exactly smooth. They went because they were obedient citizens and may have been the ones to teach their son, "Render unto Caesar …" Regardless, Joseph was the unofficial midwife and had the privilege of being the first to hold the Savior of the world, an untaxable benefit, indeed.

high note or low note?

High—compliant citizens, caring partners. Together in the responsibilities as well as the joys.

your part

When there is something unpleasant to be done (say, oh, taxes or something like that) how does it get done? Is there one person in your marriage who normally bears the weight of getting that done? Does the other one help "midwife" the situation by bringing nourishment and empathy, assisting when needed, and encouraging the one who is more involved? Do you feel supported when you are the one pulling a majority of the weight?

your duet

Offer up a prayer of gratitude for having a spouse to halve the work and double the joy. (Then do your part to make it true!)

forty four

To Protect and to Serve

Joseph and Mary
(part three)

listen

*After the wise men were gone, an angel of the Lord
appeared to Joseph in a dream. "Get up! Flee to Egypt
with the child and his mother," the angel said. "Stay
there until I tell you to return, because Herod is going
to search for the child to kill him."*

That night Joseph left for Egypt with the child and Mary, his mother, and they stayed there until Herod's death. This fulfilled what the Lord had spoken through the prophet: "I called my Son out of Egypt."

When Herod died, an angel of the Lord appeared in a dream to Joseph in Egypt. "Get up!" the angel said. "Take the child and his mother back to the land of Israel, because those who were trying to kill the child are dead."

So Joseph got up and returned to the land of Israel with Jesus and his mother. But when he learned that the new ruler of Judea was Herod's son Archelaus, he was afraid to go there. Then, after being warned in a dream, he left for the region of Galilee. So the family went and lived in a town called Nazareth. This fulfilled what the prophets had said: "He will be called a Nazarene." (Matt. 2:13–15, 19–23 NLT)

our part

Interesting note: Once the angel appeared to Mary with the news that she was going to be the mother of the Savior of the world, that was the last experience she had with angelic visitations. The subsequent appearances by angelic messengers were only to Joseph and only with warnings about how to protect Jesus. There was a definite role given to Mary (to nurture and care for the baby) and a definite role given to Joseph (to protect and defend his family). Although there had been a birth in a manger and a visitation by shepherds and wise men, there was now a warning to take an unscheduled trip to a foreign country. The world is a dangerous place. There are people who do not have your family's best interest at heart. The threat level was extremely high because Jesus' birth represented a political threat to Herod's reign, and Herod would stop at nothing (national fratricide of all baby boys under the age of two) to deter any threat to his throne. By this time Joseph may have come to understand that this would be his destiny—to be a one-man security detail for the tiny treasure entrusted to his care. And although he was not the biological father of Jesus, his protector instinct was working just fine.

high note or low note?

Joseph accepting his role as earthly father to a child of heaven? Mary accepting her husband's role in the marriage as protector, trusting his leadership—wouldn't we all love to adapt this well?

your part

Certain things usually come with the territory, but transitions in life usually come with fits and starts. Talk about some times in your marriage when it seemed like you were required to move into a new role and it felt like you might have been grinding a few gears before you engaged the clutch. How did your spouse's response help you through that time?

your duet

Think about the changes that you can anticipate in the next five years of your life together. Pray for your spouse, that God will help them adapt quickly to the new roles that these changes can thrust on them. Ask God to make you an encourager in the times of transition.

forty five

No Excuses

Joseph and Mary
(part four)

listen

Eight days later, when the baby was circumcised,
he was named Jesus, the name given him by the angel
even before he was conceived.

Then it was time for their purification offering, as
required by the law of Moses after the birth of a child;
so his parents took him to Jerusalem to present him

to the Lord. The law of the Lord says, "If a woman's
first child is a boy, he must be dedicated to the LORD."
So they offered the sacrifice required in the law of
the Lord—"either a pair of turtledoves or two young
pigeons."

When Jesus' parents had fulfilled all the
requirements of the law of the Lord, they returned
home to Nazareth in Galilee. There the child grew up
healthy and strong. He was filled with wisdom, and
God's favor was on him. (Luke 2:21–24, 39–40 NLT)

our part

Some moments reveal character in Technicolor. Though
Joseph and Mary were humble of means, they were
committed to doing the best by each other and by their
child. The pair of pigeons was the offering of the poor, but
their hearts were rich in the heritage of their faith. Joseph
and Mary were establishing their family life by following
the law and doing all they could with what they had where
they were to obey God. It would have been simple for them
to excuse themselves from their duties by rationalizing that

Jesus was, after all, the Son of God and perfect and sinless, so why bother dedicating Jesus back to God when that was where He had just come from? But Mary and Joseph wanted to do things the right way. They wanted to live up to the task they had been given. They wanted to be the kind of parents who provided a place where a boy could grow up "strong in body and wise in spirit."

And the grace of God was on Him—and them.

high note or low note?

Unity in purpose, dedication in their call to raise this child to the best of their abilities—high.

your part

It is human nature to make excuses, especially since we rely on God's grace every day of our lives. Take this moment to talk about an area where you want to come up in your commitment level and stop making excuses. Isn't your marriage and family worth a "no excuses" kind of life? Give your spouse permission to hold you accountable for your decision to give your best.

your duet

Ask God to give you the strength to make a home where everyone who lives there can flourish, because it is a place where people do what is right and do not make excuses.

I Thought He Was with You

Joseph and Mary
(part five)

listen

Every year Jesus' parents traveled to Jerusalem for the Feast of Passover. When he was twelve years old, they went up as they always did for the Feast. When it was over and they left for home, the child Jesus stayed behind in Jerusalem, but his parents didn't know it. Thinking he was somewhere in the company of pilgrims, they journeyed for a whole day and then

began looking for him among relatives and neighbors.
When they didn't find him, they went back to
Jerusalem looking for him.

The next day they found him in the Temple seated
among the teachers, listening to them and asking
questions. The teachers were all quite taken with him,
impressed with the sharpness of his answers. But his
parents were not impressed; they were upset and hurt.

His mother said, "Young man, why have you done
this to us? Your father and I have been half out of our
minds looking for you."

He said, "Why were you looking for me? Didn't you
know that I had to be here, dealing with the things of
my Father?" But they had no idea what he was talking
about.

So he went back to Nazareth with them, and lived
obediently with them. His mother held these things
dearly, deep within herself. (Luke 2:41–51)

our part

If you have children, you will have played out this scenario at least once.

"I thought he rode with you."

"No, I thought he said he was riding back with you."

"We left the kid at church!"

A round of blame ensues, if only to cover up the panic you feel at your inadequate parenting and to have a place to displace the mounting tension as you wonder if your child will still be there when you finally get back.

And then—ah, relief when they are exactly where you left them.

Mary takes the usual mom approach: "Why did you do this to us?"

And Jesus answers with a statement that seems confusing to them both about "dealing with the things of my Father." Apparently they couldn't hear the capital F in "Father" because the next statement is, "But they had no idea what he was talking about."

Were they really that far from the manger that they did not remember His mission?

We would do well to keep in mind (in the midst of

the myriad parenting responsibilities that consume us regularly) that, like Jesus, our children are entrusted to us for just a short while and then we release them to go about doing their own things of their Father.

high note or low note?

The panic was understandable; their confusion totally understandable. Their dedication to their child— unquestionable. They were busy parents trying to keep up with a son who marched to a different drummer. High.

your part

If you are parents, or are planning to bring children into your family, it is imperative that you ask yourself what your end goal is so you can keep it in mind as the years and responsibilities become more and more complicated. Talk about what you can see your children doing as young adults. Share your opinions and come to a consensus on the kinds of values you believe God wants you to teach them.

your duet

To ensure that you don't lose your sense of being a couple in the middle of all the parenting, plan at least a few days every year to engage in empty-nest practice. This is a week (or weekend, if you can't take a full week) you set aside to vacation together without your children. (But don't let that include accidentally leaving your children at church, or anywhere else for that matter.) Remember that this configuration (the two of you) was how the marriage started and, if all your children successfully launch from your nest, it will be once again someday. This empty-nest practice is important so that you don't end up strangers in the same house someday.

forty seven

Where Your Treasure Is

Chuza and Joanna

listen

Joanna, wife of Chuza, Herod's manager; and Susanna—along with many others ... used their considerable means to provide for the company.

Mary Magdalene, Joanna, Mary the mother of James, and the other women with them kept telling these things to the apostles, but the apostles didn't believe a word of it, thought they were making it all up. (Luke 8:3; 24:10–11)

our part

Someone said, "When God blesses you, He rarely has you in mind." (If you're the one who said it, please email us so we can give you credit.) This Scripture tells us that Chuza was Herod's manager. This was a man who was in a place of political power and had the paycheck that went with it. He and his wife, Joanna, were financial supporters of Jesus and the twelve disciples. Some people are willing to give of their wealth, but not of their time and attention, but this couple was available in all three categories. They were followers of Christ in life and were among the devastated when He was crucified. This account tells us that Joanna was with the women who went to tend to the body of Jesus and experienced the elation of being told by the angels that Jesus had risen from the dead. The women told the apostles—who didn't believe them—but they knew what they had seen with their own eyes. It is of note that Joanna and Chuza were dwelling squarely between two worlds: following Jesus, while working for the people who wanted to kill their Messiah. But they proved that a person will follow where their treasure is—even beyond a grave.

high note or low note?

An example of using your wealth to support things that you believe in. High.

your part

What do you do with your wealth? (And you can't say you don't have any. Everyone has something.) Do you take a portion of the money you are blessed to earn and support a local church, or a global mission project, or something else you believe in? It's easy to give lip service, but it's meaningful and empowering when we open our wallets and prove it. It is a biblical principle that a couple who gives generously will also receive.

your duet

Do you feel that it's time to increase your giving as a couple? Find a ministry or cause that tugs at your heart and begin to invest in it financially.

forty eight

Real-Estate Roulette

Ananias and Sapphira

listen

But a man named Ananias—his wife, Sapphira,
conniving in this with him—sold a piece of land,
secretly kept part of the price for himself, and then
brought the rest to the apostles and made an offering
of it.

Peter said, "Ananias, how did Satan get you to lie to
the Holy Spirit and secretly keep back part of the price
of the field? Before you sold it, it was all yours, and

*after you sold it, the money was yours to do with as you
wished. So what got into you to pull a trick like this?
You didn't lie to men but to God."*

*Ananias, when he heard those words, fell down dead.
That put the fear of God into everyone who heard of it.
The younger men went right to work and wrapped him
up, then carried him out and buried him.*

*Not more than three hours later, his wife, knowing
nothing of what had happened, came in. Peter said,
"Tell me, were you given this price for your field?"*

"Yes," she said, "that price."

*Peter responded, "What's going on here that you
connived to conspire against the Spirit of the Master?
The men who buried your husband are at the door,
and you're next." No sooner were the words out of his
mouth than she also fell down, dead. When the young
men returned they found her body. They carried her
out and buried her beside her husband. (Acts 5:1–10)*

our part

The lying would have been bad enough. It was the collusion that was the real killer.

The ingredients of this real-estate offering gone wrong—a heart that devises wicked schemes and a lying tongue—are listed in Proverbs as two of the seven things God despises (along with a proud look, hands that shed innocent blood, feet that rush to evil, one who gives lies under oath, and one who stirs up dissent). We suppose one would be enough to get you in trouble, but any combination of that list seems to put you into some seriously deep God-trouble. The apostle Peter discerned that Ananias was not on the up-and-up regarding his percentage that he brought as an offering. This was in the Acts 2 days when the Bible tells us that they "had all things in common" to support the apostles and the early church (see Acts 2:43–45). As Peter pointed out, this certainly was not a requirement, and they could have freely given any amount they wished. The word *integrity* comes from *wholeness* or *of a whole cloth*, meaning that there are no seams, no divisions, no places where something has been pieced together. It is the same from one side to the other.

Ananias and Sapphira certainly had a seam in their moral fabric because they wanted to appear more spiritual and generous than they actually were and didn't mind allowing other people to think they had completely liquidated their assets and were relying on God for their future. This kind of spiritual fronting often masks a marriage with no real substance and a casual regard for matters of integrity. They had already written the end of their story. It just came a lot quicker than they expected.

high note or low note?

They got carried out like downed gunslingers in a saloon. Pretty low.

your part

Could your marriage be categorized as one of integrity? If people were to witness your life inside your home with the curtains drawn, would they say, "Yes. Those are the people I know," or would they say, "Those are not the same people at all!"? When our lives are integrity filled, there is nothing we are conspiring to pass off as "who we are." We simply are who we are, all the time. This is how people know they can depend on us, how our families know they can trust us, and how we deal truthfully in our spiritual lives.

your duet

At the same time, but on separate sheets of paper, write down any areas in your life and marriage you feel could be more transparent and integrity filled. These have to be common to the marriage and not just specific to your spouse. You can't begin any sentence with "I wish that _____ (spouse) would _____."

Share them with each other, then seal them in an envelope with today's date. Agree to pray about them and look at them six months from now to see if you have made strides toward a more integrity-filled marriage just by being aware of these areas.

Entertained but Unchanged

Felix and Drusilla

listen

A few days later Felix and his wife, Drusilla,
who was Jewish, sent for Paul and listened to him
talk about a life of believing in Jesus Christ. As Paul
continued to insist on right relations with God and his
people, about a life of moral discipline and the coming
Judgment, Felix felt things getting a little too close for
comfort and dismissed him. "That's enough for today.
I'll call you back when it's convenient." At the same
time he was secretly hoping that Paul would offer him

a substantial bribe. These conversations were repeated frequently.

After two years of this, Felix was replaced by Porcius Festus. Still playing up to the Jews and ignoring justice, Felix left Paul in prison. (Acts 24:24–27)

our part

Paul was a feisty apostle. Because he had traipsed through the halls of power in both the political and religious realms, he had no level of discomfort ministering there. So he would seek to speak to the hearts of rulers about Jesus Christ at every opportunity. In the book of Acts, we encounter Felix and Drusilla; Felix was the procurator of Judea, and Drusilla was the daughter of King Agrippa and knew a thing or two about how wealth and power could serve you well. Paul's repeated appearances entertained them, but they could not bear the fact that their lives would have to change should they choose to follow Christ. So repeatedly they would call for him to preach to them and then leave him in prison a few months. This went on for a couple of years. They had all the knowledge they needed to enter into a life that would bring them forgiveness, grace, and eternal life (not to mention poverty and certain instantaneous removal from office). This constant quest for knowledge without change is not limited to Felix and Drusilla. How many financial-management seminars have you been to and yet your finances remain a mess? Have you been to marital tune-up retreats only to slip back into the old patterns? *The Message* Bible sums up Felix's default stance as "playing up … and ignoring justice"—a sad bottom line. In this way Felix and Drusilla were like a lot of couples who want a faith that merely informs their lives, not transforms it.

high note or low note?

Because of their inability to commit, we cannot acquit. Low.

your part

We know that a life of faith requires action. You can't just read and hear and learn and consider. You must accept and do. What truth have you encountered recently together that you both feel impressed to commit to and act on but you just can't seem to move into the "action mode"? What do you think is stopping you?

your duet

It is a privilege to pray for each other. Ask God to help your spouse move beyond knowledge to action in areas where it may require sacrifice from both of you. Pray that this will bring about changes in the world for rightness and justice that will last forever.

fifty

We'll Leave the Light On

Aquila and Priscilla
(part one)

listen

After Athens, Paul went to Corinth. That is where
he discovered Aquila, a Jew born in Pontus, and
his wife, Priscilla. They had just arrived from Italy,
part of the general expulsion of Jews from Rome
ordered by Claudius. Paul moved in with them,
and they worked together at their common trade of
tentmaking. But every Sabbath he was at the meeting

place, doing his best to convince both Jews and Greeks about Jesus.

He stayed another year and a half, faithfully teaching the Word of God to the Corinthians. (Acts 18:1–4, 11)

our part

Those welcoming Italians. They might have just landed in Corinth, but they were willing to give an itinerant missionary/tentmaker a spare bedroom. And once the bedroom was opened, why not just let the non-Jewish believers in—and, while we're at it—let's have a house-church meet here, too! When you choose to embrace a spirit of hospitality, your slogan isn't "the more, the merrier," it's "the more, the ministry-er." They did not open their home merely to make it a showcase for their fine decorating or culinary skills. Their focus was on the people who were in their sphere of influence and how best to facilitate meeting their spiritual needs. Sure, it would have been more convenient to come in after a long day of making tents together, close the door behind them, eat a quiet dinner, and call it a day. Who among us hasn't been really glad that you didn't have to face your coworkers at home? But they knew their inclusiveness was essential to the mission of reaching their city and beyond. And verse 11 tells us that Paul stayed with them for a year and a half—no "fish and guests stink after three days" rule here. Only the rule of love. And some good ol' Italian hospitality.

high note or low note?

A couple who welcome people into their home and invest in the lives of others will find themselves enriched in some way.

your part

Would you say your home is one of hospitality and openness? Have you invited persons who are not in your family into your home in the last month? The last six months? If not, why not?

your duet

Hospitality is a practice. It's something you choose to do. It's not about the food or the amenities, it's about having an open heart and sharing your life with others. Make a pact to up your "HQ" (hospitality quotient) from whatever level you are currently on.

Long-Term, High-Yield
Investments

Aquila and Priscilla
(part two)

listen

They landed in Ephesus, where Priscilla and Aquila got off and stayed. Paul left the ship briefly to go to the meeting place and preach to the Jews.

A man named Apollos came to Ephesus. He was a Jew, born in Alexandria, Egypt, and a terrific speaker, eloquent and powerful in his preaching of the Scriptures. He was well-educated in the way of the Master and fiery in his enthusiasm. Apollos was accurate in everything he taught about Jesus up to a point, but he only went as far as the baptism of John. He preached with power in the meeting place. When Priscilla and Aquila heard him, they took him aside and told him the rest of the story.

When Apollos decided to go on to Achaia province, his Ephesian friends gave their blessing and wrote a letter of recommendation for him, urging the disciples there to welcome him with open arms. The welcome paid off: Apollos turned out to be a great help to those who had become believers through God's immense generosity. He was particularly effective in public debate with the Jews as he brought out proof after convincing proof from the Scriptures that Jesus was in fact God's Messiah. (Acts 18:19–20, 24–28)

our part

The lives of this couple were like the tides of the ocean—let people in, send people out, let people in, send people out. Not only were Priscilla and Aquila gracious and open with their home, they were open and gracious to mentor and invest in the lives of others. When they encountered Apollos in Ephesus and heard him speak, they were convinced that he had great talent but was not telling the whole story. It is indicative of their generous hearts that they did not tsk-tsk and leave Apollos to continue on his path to be only half as effective as he could be. They cared enough to take him aside (they did not humiliate him by correcting him publicly) and provide him with the information he needed to move on to his next assignment. They also felt strongly enough about his abilities that they gave him a "To Whom It May Concern—Give This Guy a Hearing" letter. Their willingness to get involved and mentor a younger-in-the-faith brother resulted in many people believing in Jesus. They may have been in the business of making tents, but their passion was touching lives.

high note or low note?

One of the strongest stories of partnership with a purpose in the Bible. High.

your part

One of the hallmarks of spiritual maturity is taking on some mentoring relationships, individually and as a couple. It requires us to be transparent in our own lives when we pour into the lives of others. Regardless of where you are on your path, there is always someone who is just a little behind you on their journey who needs the wisdom, encouragement, and perspective that you possess.

your duet

If mentoring has not been a priority for you as a couple, ask God to reveal people to whom your mentorship would be an important and potentially life-changing investment of your time and energy.

fifty two

Laying It on the Line

Aquila and Priscilla
(part three)

listen

Say hello to Priscilla and Aquila, who have worked hand in hand with me in serving Jesus. They once put their lives on the line for me. And I'm not the only one grateful to them. All the non-Jewish gatherings of believers also owe them plenty, to say nothing of the church that meets in their house. (Rom. 16:3–5)

Say hello to Priscilla and Aquila. (2 Tim. 4:19)

our part

Paul was all about the shout-out. He was quick in his writings to give one to people who meant a lot to him and impacted his life. In this shout-out, he elaborates on Priscilla and Aquila (don't you just love that their names rhyme?) and their no-holds-barred commitment. They have since returned to Rome, but Paul wants to let them know how much they mean to him. He says that they put their lives where their lips were and faced personal danger in helping him. It is one thing to say that you believe in a person or a cause; it's quite another to risk because of it. People often say there is very little they would give their life for, but the truth is that we are, in fact, exchanging our lives for something. For some it is the pursuit of money or position or standing in the community. For some it is the pure thrill of acquisition. For others it is their children. But we are all exchanging units of our lives (time) for something. You are literally giving your life for something. Make sure it is something you believe in.

high note or low note?

High. Commitment requires risk, and they embraced this aspect of their lives with complete unity (notice that they are always referenced in the Bible as a unit).

your part

The truth is that most of the things we spend our time and energy on won't even be around a hundred years from now—so what are you doing as a couple that will count then? What are your "life or death" causes? Do you have any that you share as a couple? Would anyone be able to give you this sort of shout-out? For whom have you risked?

your duet

This might be a good time to implement the 10-10-10 test in your marriage. When faced with a decision or situation, it's good to get perspective by asking yourself, "Will this matter in 10 minutes? 10 months? 10 years?"

encore

What has been will be again, what has been done will
be done again; there is nothing new under the sun.
(Eccl. 1:9 NIV)

After reading this mixed bag of couples throughout the Bible, it is intriguing, indeed, that Paul
would equate the relationship between Christ
and the church to that of a married couple. But that is
precisely the word picture he chose to describe the relationship. The intimacy. The mystery. The power. There is
nothing like the coming together of a man and a woman
for purposes beyond their own individual interests.
Creating something larger than the sum of the parts,
something of lasting legacy.

As the verse from Ecclesiastes tells us, we are not the
first to encounter these struggles in our relationships—
nor will we be the last. And, because we believe that life

is too short to make all your own mistakes, we can learn from others. Experience is a good teacher, but the lessons are hard. And the consequences are long lasting.

Our prayer is that, after reading about these couples and the hardships they faced and their resulting decisions, you would feel more careful *and* more hopeful about your marriage. We believe that God's desire for you and your marriage is to have true intimacy and not to merely coexist but rather to truly appreciate each other and grow together.

Now go sing your own duet.